The Wells

A Book of Se... Inspirations

By Anna Franklin and Pamela Harvey

Illustrated by Helen Field

The Wellspring
A Book of Seasonal
Inspirations

©1999 Anna Franklin & Pamela Harvey

ISBN 186163 078 6

ALL RIGHTS RESERVED

No part of this publication may be reproduced, stored in a retrieval system or transmitted in any form or by any means, electronic, mechanical, photocopying, scanning, recording or otherwise without the prior written permission of the author and the publisher.

Internal illustrations by Helen Field
Cover design by Paul Mason

Published by:

Capall Bann Publishing
Freshfields
Chieveley
Berks
RG20 8TF

Contents

Chapter One Imbolc The First Stirrings of Spring   3
    Rowan Tree Pathworking   3
    The Plough Rite   6
    Eve and the Goddess   7
    Imbolc Herb Craft   10
    The Festival of Brighid   13
    Imbolc Rite   15
    The Wellspring   18

Chapter Two Ostara The Vernal Equinox   23
    Gorse Tree Pathworking   25
    Flower Ritual   26
    The Hare   27
    Ostara Herb Craft   33
    Altar Decorations   34
    The Serpent and the Egg   37
    Drawing Down the Sun Ritual   40
    Rite For Ostara   41

Chapter Three Beltane The Coming of Summer   45
    Beltane Herb Craft   47
    Rite For Beltane   50
    Contacting the Goddess Within   51
    Life on Earth   52
    The Sacred Animals of Beltane   54

Chapter Four Coamhain The Golden Season   59
    Coamhain Herb Craft   62
    Coamhain Ritual   67
    Oak Tree Pathworking   69
    The Journey That Never Ends   73
    The Bee - Avatar of the Summer Goddess   75
    Bee Pathworking   79

Chapter Five Lughnasa Season of Summer Ripeness 81
    The Stag   83
    Stag Pathworking   87
    The Warrior   89
    Lughnasa Herb Craft   90
    Rite For Lughnasa   95

Blessing the Grain Ritual	97
La Mas Nbhal	99
Chapter Six Herfest The Time of Completion	**102**
Herfest Herb Craft	103
Blessing of the Harvest Ritual	108
The Salmon	109
Salmon Pathworking	113
The Corn Dolly	114
The Cauldron	115
Consecrating a Cauldron	117
Waves	118
Persephone	119
Chapter Seven Samhain Hunter's Moon Meditation	**129**
Candles	131
Making Candles	133
Consecrating Candles	134
November Ritual	134
Purification Ritual	135
Imprisonment	136
The Wall	138
Rite For Samhain	140
Chapter Eight Yule The Midwinter Solstice	**143**
The Wassail	146
Holly, Ivy, Evergreen	147
Yule Ritual For Two Celebrants	150
Yule Pathworking	151
Solo Yule Ritual	152
Yuletide in a Modern World	153
Group Rite For Yule	155

Chapter One

Imbolc

PRAYER TO ATHENA
Just to be me alone
That I will not be taught.
You of whom the myth was sung,
From the brow of Zeus had sprung,
Goddess of Thought,
Listen now to my plea
Not to be merely me-
Let me be more of thee, who Wisdom sought.

We who belong to you
And from each other share
That gift of Inspiration
To which Reason is the heir,
May we always know
Though we may creature be,
Yet we are Thought.

Imagination thus
Revealed in you to be
From the Divinity, given to us,
We may be no greater thing,
-If seeming trivial and small-
Than to be thought by One
Who would think All.
PH

* Festival of Brighid *

The First Stirrings of Spring

Imbolc, celebrated in the snowy depths of early February, marks the very first awakening of spring. The bare arms of winter trees begin to redden with sap and the first snowdrops poke their heads from the cold earth. The Crone Goddess of winter sheds her dark mantle and becomes the young Maiden of Spring, full of the promise of the year. With the white wand she carries she brings life back to the dead land, quickening life in the womb of Mother Earth.

Animals begin to shake off their winter sleep and emerge from hibernation. Young lambs are born and nurtured. The ploughs are brought out and blessed, and the first furrow is tilled.

In the Craft we celebrate Imbolc as the festival of the Maiden Goddess, who is called Brighid, Athene, Arianrhod, Diana, Artemis, Persephone, Minerva, Isis and many other names. She is the White Goddess of Inspiration, the Muse of the bard, the Lady of Magic, the Healer, the Guardian of the Hearth. On her wheel she spins the cosmos, her cup is the womb from which we are all born, the grail of wisdom, and her mirror reflects the truth and shows us things yet to come.

Imbolc is the festival of womankind, when women gather to celebrate their gifts of creativity and nurturing on all levels, and offer them to the Goddess.
AF

Rowan Tree Pathworking

Relax.

You find yourself, on a cold day at the beginning of February, on a hill. It is approaching dawn and there are patches of snow amidst the tufts of grass.

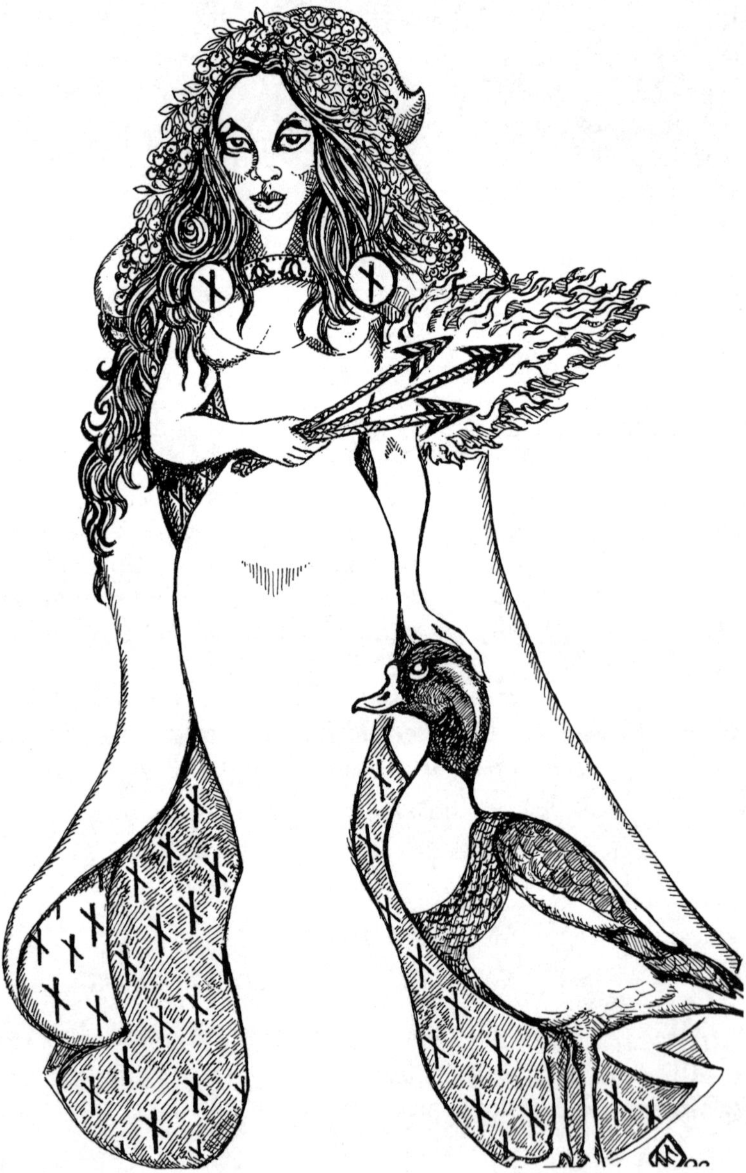

On top of the hill is a grove of trees and you begin climbing towards it. Between the branches, you can just make out the flickering of a fire.

As you approach the grove you can see that the trees are rowan, the Druid's tree, their greyish trunks reaching up towards the darkened sky, still hung with a few bunches of berries, red as flame. You reach up and pluck a cluster of them, and you can see that the base of each berry is marked with a five pointed star, a pentacle, the mark of the Goddess. You tuck the berries into the collar of your coat.

Thus protected, you enter the grove. The rowan trees surround a circle of nineteen stones.

In the centre of the circle is a brazier, burning with a bright flame. Fire-threads of sparks leap up from it.

Seated by the fire is an old woman, cloaked and hooded in black. She is spinning thread from a quickly revolving spinning wheel. The threads are luminous and she collects them on a spindle made of rowan wood.

'I have kept the flames of life burning throughout the winter,' she says.

You wonder what it is that she is spinning. You may go up to her and ask her what you will.

After a time she takes a cup from beneath her cloak, a grail. Taking the berries from your collar, she squeezes the juice into the cup. You are surprised as the foaming red liquid fills the grail.

She holds the cup towards you and says *'This is the food of Gods and initiates. The blood red gives life and vitality. The rowan gives visions.'*

You take the cup and drink from it. As you do, the spinning wheel begins to turn of its own accord, and with it the grove. You are at the hub of a spinning wheel. The wheel of the year itself. As the sun rises over the heel stone winter begins to melt into spring.

You look back at the old woman. She throws off her cloak and is dressed in glowing white, bathed in the light of the risen sun. Her face is no longer wrinkled and drawn, but shining with youth and vitality. Bright red hair ripples down her back like tongues of fire. In her hand is a quiver containing three arrows of rowan wood, each tipped with a living flame. She laughs.

As she walks through the grove snowdrops appear in her footsteps. As she passes the trees their branches swell with buds.

She smiles at you and you feel life and energy quicken within you.

When you are ready, thank the Lady and let the scene fade around you and return yourself to waking consciousness.

AF

The Plough Rite

In ancient times, after the rebirth of the sun at the winter solstice, the ploughs and agricultural implements would be blessed and prepared ready for the work to come when the weather picked up. Chanting, dancing and singing would drive away the spirits of winter and offerings were made for a successful harvest.

In Christian times this festival was called Plough Monday, and falls on the first Monday after the Epiphany, marking the return to work after the holidays. A plough was decorated and blessed and processed through the village.

Now the sun has been reborn we can look forward to the spring, though the weather in January and February is often the coldest part of the year. In the depths of winter it is a time to hope and look forward.

Take out some of your gardening equipment, even if you only have houseplants you will probably have little trowels and watering cans. Clean the implements thoroughly and decorate them with ribbons and any flowers you can find. Prepare your sacred space and lay them before the altar.

"I call upon you God and Goddess of the harvest to witness that I dedicate these tools in your honour. In this time of dark and cold, we trust that the spring will return, that the earth will become green once more, that the flowers and fruits will grow. With these tools I will work the earth and bring forth your bounty and your harvest."

Sprinkle the tools with water to purify them and lay your hands on them in blessing.

"Lord and Lady, be with us throughout the year and grant us your blessings".

The cakes and wine are taken and the sacred space banished.
AF

Eve and the Goddess
Somewhere in the female psyche the symbol of wayward womanhood dissolves into the mystery of the Virgin Goddess, retreating into a lost world where both sexuality and innocence dwell. In many legends female divinities kept both these aspects as one - for example, Aphrodite was said to

renew her virginity in the sea, unchanging scene of her spirit being.

In the early dawn of humanity women were believed to have been chosen by the gods as mates *'the sons of god saw the daughters of men that they were fair, and took them wives of all they chose'* as stated in the Bible. The god Manannan was amorously inclined to mortal women at times, and the Greek god Zeus gave his favours to mortals and goddesses as and when appropriate.

These days the media tells us that women are inclined to be disillusioned with marriage. Perhaps they wonder if they have made the right choice, or somewhere the grass is greener, or they simply do not need to put up with the inevitable irritations of sharing daily life with another human being. We live in an age when women can earn as much or more than men, when they can make their own way in the world, and where they are sophisticated and educated. Men- who needs then? Well, perhaps sometimes...

We are not all alike of course. Opportunities for equal status there may be, but not all of us have the confidence, or the success in education, to take advantage of them. Also, we are not all ambitious, or potential managers or leaders. Such qualities- dare one whisper it- are still often, though by no means not always, the characteristics of men. However, such women as do not possess such qualities in abundance are made to feel ashamed of the fact. At one time we would have been regarded as demure, as long as we adhered to the strict sexual moral code of past days concerning the fair gender. If at all wayward, the less domineering type of female would have been regarded by men as available. Times have not changed much in some ways, but at least women now have the law on their side.

We must hope for a society where we are valued as intelligent human beings, where we perhaps may discern in the coming era the lost world of the gods. Goddesses have usually managed to have equal rights to life and worship. But legend puts both men and women in a place well below divinity- that may have been its object, no matter what the form. But in order to gain the worship of the masses, the gods and goddesses had to be worthy of it- to be the focus of the deeper yearnings of the human heart. The spirit rules the ultimate sense of longing as the sun shines upon the earth. In the moon there is the mysterious union of longing and its objective. If we are not spiritual beings we might as well forget finding a meaning to life. Emotions and fantasies need this nucleus at the centre of their fire, the depths of their dream.

Moral codes vary- the most encouraging thing about them is that they exist. We live in a tolerant age, but not without common sense. Even if no-one has the right to tell anyone else how to live- or love. Somewhere, somehow, we are something of everything; Aphrodite Urania and Aphrodite Pandemos; with latent, or actual independent spirits like some of the Celtic goddesses, or pliant, recognising the heroic in men, as perhaps Rhiannon did with Manawydden.

We know the age of glamourie is never lost; to the Faery race even withered autumn leaves could be transformed into beauty. In the depths of the dream the dark realty of the Goddess still calls to Eve that her world is too material, has forgotten the ebb and flow of the quantum universe. The Leanne Sidhe still haunts mankind-the subtle power of the feminine exists. Men, when confident in their long traditional role in society, might feel as Narcissus who loved his own image in the forest pool more than the elusive charm of the nymph Echo. Her voice and vision haunted him down the valley of Time...

Our personalities may imitate the many-hued robe of Isis, in our lesser manner, if only we can find our inner and outer Sun.
PH

IMBOLC HYMN TO ISIS

Oh, how dark was the dawning of this Age
That gave my trembling wish its heritage;
In disillusion, doubt, a woman sad
Sought Life's illusive Wisdom lotus bud.

Now I look back and think about the way;
Perhaps it leads to bright and golden day.
Through mists of sorrow now the light shines clear,
Though distant, showing ending to my fear.

The Earth is restless, many cannot find
Within debate and conflict, peace of mind;
Yet we were born beyond the path of Time
In Knowledge ever Present and sublime.

So give me know the hope I offered you,
That my immortal dream can yet come true;
For I would share its meaning in this hour
With those who need assurance of its Power,
That from the Earthly seed I sowed can bloom
The glowing Sunflowers from an empty tomb.
PH

Imbolc Herb Craft

This is a bleak time of year when the weather is at its worst and coldest. Snow often covers the ground and there is little fresh food to be found. At this time we are using stored produce, such as old potatoes and onions, and preserved and dried foods such as beans and lentils. There should still be parsnips and leeks in the ground, and if you are lucky some early green shoots of plants such as chickweed [Stellaria media] which is one of the first plants to return and its pale green stems may be found spreading along the ground, heralding the renewal of the land. This can be made into a tea, incorporated in soups, or used as green salad.

Imbolc is sometimes called 'the time of the green shoots' though the first sign of spring is really the reddening of tree twigs from the rising sap. Any young edible shoots are good at this time to remind us that the earth is about to blossom forth, if you have no access to wild ones, try making some of your own. Take some mung or aduki beans and place them in a jam jar with some blotting paper soaked in water. Pierce the lid of the jar and turn it occasionally until the beans have sprouted.

Birch is associated with purification and its branches are used in a country ritual for driving out the old year. The word birch derives from a root meaning 'bright' or 'shining'. White trees being used to drive out black magic and the dark. The appearance of birch leaves marks the beginning of the agricultural year. Brighid's wand is made of birch or willow.

The willow is associated with the feminine, water, tides, the moon and witchcraft. It is sacred to the Moon Goddess and is a tree of bards and poets.

The rowan, or quickbeam is associated with the quickening of life. It is further associated with the feast of Brighid as its Irish poetic name is Luisiu Orflame, referring to the constantly burning flame of Brighid.
AF

BRIGHID CAKES
1 lb. plain flour
4 oz margarine
4oz sugar
2 oz chopped peel

¾ pint milk
Pinch of salt
1 tsp. bicarbonate of soda
1 tsp. cream of tartar
4 oz sultanas

Method
Sieve the flour and salt, cream of tartar and bicarbonate of soda into a bowl. Rub in the margarine, then add the sugar, peel and sultana. Add the milk and knead into a dough. Place in a greased 7" tin and bake in a hot oven at 200ºC/400ºF/gas mark 6 for 60 minutes. Turn the oven down to 180ºC/350ºF/gas mark 4 and bake for another 30 minutes. Turn out and cut into smaller pieces to serve.

IMBOLC INCENSE
1 part willow wood
1 part crushed rowan berries
½ part periwinkle flowers
½ part lily of the valley flowers
2 parts benzoin

Method
Blend together and burn on charcoal.

BRIGHID INCENSE
1 part crushed rowan berries
¼ part blackberry leaves
1 part birch bark
1 part willow bark
½ part bistort root
1 part oak bark
½ part snowdrop flowers
¼ part flax flowers

Method
Blend together and burn on charcoal

The Festival of Brighid

Imbolc is also the festival of the Celtic goddess Brighid, Christianised as St. Brigit or St. Bride. Christian apologists gave her the role of midwife to the virgin Mary and in Celtic areas she is still deemed to be the saint who should be invoked at Childbirth.

In Celtic legend Brighid was the daughter of the great god Dagda and was the Celtic counterpart of Athene. She is a triple fire goddess and her name comes from Breo-saigit which means 'fiery arrow'. Hers are the three fire arrows of inspiration, healing and the hearth or forge. She is the muse of poets who lived under her patronage, and who carried a golden branch hung with small bells in her honour. She is the goddess of healing wells where offerings were left to solicit healing. She was also a goddess of the hearth fire and the forge, patroness of the magician-smith who transformed, by his alchemy, elements of the underworld into beautiful or useful objects.

Her cult centre was in Kildare [Cilldare -'Temple of the oak'] where a fire was perpetually kept burning by nineteen virgins. Each maiden tended the fire for one day of a twenty day cycle and on the twentieth day Brighid herself was said to tend the fire. The flame was concealed behind a thorn hedge and any man who entered was said to either go mad or burst into flames.

The moon's progress through the heavens repeats itself every nineteen years. Many stone circles have nineteen stones, some seem to have a vacant space for a missing twentieth, echoing the cycle of Brighid and her nineteen maidens. Castle Rigg stone circle is orientated to the sunrise at Imbolc.

Brighid is depicted with three objects: the mirror, the spinning wheel and the cup or grail. The mirror might identify Brighid with the Great Goddess figure who was

14

portrayed with comb and mirror [as the mermaid still is]. The mirror is used for scrying and divination. The spinning wheel is the bright spinning centre of the cosmos, dancing in the sky and also the turning of the wheel of the year, bringing life, death and rebirth. The wheel spins the threads of life and the turns bring change. The cup is the womb of the Goddess from which all things are born and from which all things are sustained, as the ewe's milk at Imbolc sustains the lambs.

Brighid is also known as the White Swan or the ancient snake and bird goddess in one form, giving her both Underworld and Overworld connections. Snakes were kept as oracles at her shrines and for a snake to emerge from hibernation at Imbolc was thought to be a very good omen for the coming year. In her death aspect she is associated with a bird of prey and is sometimes portrayed with a wolf, one of the totem guardians of Britain, ruler of the winter quarter which begins at Samhain and ends at Imbolc. February was called 'the wolf month'.

Brighid carries a white wand - a fertilising phallus without the aid of a god or male counterpart. With it she regenerates the lifeless land, bringing back the green plants and new birth amongst animals. She is said to breath 'new life into the mouth of dead winter'.

In ancient Celtic times the married women of the tribe would paint themselves with woad and go naked to the Imbolc festival site to honour the Crone Goddess, the Veiled One, while the younger women would gather gifts to offer at Brighid's shrine.

Imbolc Rite

Imbolc marks the purification of the Goddess after the birth of the young God, and the renewal of her maidenhood in the eternal cycle of Maiden, Mother and Crone. Now is the time when the earth is washed clean by the rains after the winter, and the land prepares to renew itself with the first signs of spring.

The candles and decorations are green and white. The altar is decorated with the first spring flowers and greenery, and boughs of willow wood. There is either a bonfire in the centre of the circle, or a cauldron with candles in it to represent the fire. A large dish or cauldron of water is placed near the altar. All the women prepare what is called by some 'Brighid's Bed' to which the Goddess is invited to witness the proceedings. A soft pallet is prepared and set about with candles and lamps. Everyone prepares two garlands- one representing winter [made from old Yule decorations, dead winter twigs etc. and one representing spring made from green shoots, spring flowers etc. The winter garland is worn and the spring garland kept by].

The circle is cast.

Celebrant One: "*Queen and Lady, Goddess of the Night. Secret Goddess, thy servants call upon thee, for this is the time of thy festival. Come now and enter our circle. Enter Lady, come now to thy bed and bless thy servants.*"

Celebrant Two: [Lighting the candles in cauldron]"*Let this fire in the centre of the circle represent the perpetual fire of the spirit of the Goddess. Let it be a beacon to call the Old Gods to us. The Lady's fire gives life to the strengthening sun, and to each of us. Be welcome, Hag of Winter.*"

Celebrant One: (throwing down the symbols of winter - the winter garlands) "*The dead time is past, the wheel turns towards new life and spring.*"

Celebrant Two: "*The rains of spring wash winter from the earth. They nurture the growing shoots of life as the ewe feeds the young lamb. The rains of Spring transform the Hag of Winter into the Maiden of Spring."*

She washes in the cauldron and puts on her spring garland.

Celebrant One: *"The Goddess is in every woman and man and every woman and man is part of the Goddess- let each of you wash in the pool, be purified in mind, body and spirit. Let the water transform you into a new Self, like the Maiden of Spring, ready to grow and flower with the year."*

Each washes in the cauldron, helped by the others, then puts on the spring garland. Celebrant Two then washes the crystal in the water to symbolise the spring rains washing the earth and explains the symbolism as she does so. After this each person states to the others what they have to offer to the Goddess in terms of their talents and strengths, what they have to offer the world and themselves. After this scry in the crystal, mirror or fire.

Celebrant One: [takes up the cup of wine] *"The cup is the grail of the Goddess, her womb from which we were all born. It is the cauldron of transformation where we partake of the Spirit, from which we are nurtured and fed. As we drink of this cup we share in these gifts of the Goddess."* [All drink.]

Celebrant Two: *"These cakes are from the body of the Mother Earth, our Goddess. She sustains our lives with Her gifts. As we eat of them may we partake of the love of the Goddess."*

Celebrant One: *"The Goddess has witnessed our rites and seen the truth of our hearts. Let this rite be ended in perfect love and perfect trust. Blessed Be."*

When all is done the circle is closed and the feasting begins.

AF

The Wellspring

In the fast ebbing tides of the 20th century ripples of ignorance are being disturbed. The frenetic rush to nowhere of the era of materialism exists now not only in its own whirlpool but in a deeper, wider lake of unknown proportions. Where the stars are reflected, and the secret Universe shifts the folds of its dark gossamer curtain.

People captivated by new ideas from other parts of the world, meditations, exercises or more arcane philosophies than they have encountered before may forget that still 'out there' in earth's teeming wilderness, the bustling towns, the bursting cities, there is a frequently suppressed but dire hunger. A need to know- what is life? Where, if anywhere, is it going? Is there something that guides? Am I a small boat cast adrift on a sea of indifference? How can my life possibly matter in a cosmos of billions of worlds?

Religions address these questions, as they always have. But to many in the Euro-transatlantic civilisation, this flame has faltered so much in the winds of materialism that it is either just a memory- or a dream. To many of us, humankind stands alone. The individual feels 'I am my last frontier'. Our lives just part of a repeated programme on the DNA computer. Not everyone finds it easy, or even possible, to be lifted into a deeper, higher awareness by revelations of the old, or new traditions. Some humans are just prosaically minded, others worried and preoccupied with urgent everyday necessities or insoluble personal problems. Some have very little imagination.

I was recently handed a leaflet by a Christian group. I am a Pagan, but personally regard Jesus as an expression of the Sun God at the deepest level. The small leaflet stated categorically that people were mistaken to think that there was any other way to the Divine except the Christ approach. This is a view that is not held by other, more open-minded folk of that faith. But I felt it to be very off putting to those of us humans who are looking for something to reassure, someone to hold our hand. Whether we like the idea or not, our planet is looking outward; television/satellite pictures have shown us our island Earth, beautiful, fecund, calm- at a distance. Mother Earth has given her children priceless gifts. If we can sense her maternal arms around us, we can be comforted. But in this raucous age it is not easy. We need to share our perceptions, our thoughts.

At the heart of imagination, or sensed in meditation, or diffused in contemplation, is the lost world of All-knowing. Of sensing a presence, a personal Someone.

There must be many gods and many goddesses. If only in that this implies that the Wellspring of Being has many fountains whose avatars are the Waters of Life. The stream is all One; the Universe drinks from the Source that quenches the thirst of ignorance and despair. Our own personalities are no two the same. I feel that Divinity needs to be only Itself. It may differ quite considerably in aspects, in types of personality expressing alternative characteristics; it may be proud, strong, tough- or gentle, responsive, understanding. All of this, perhaps, in male or female form, or no form at all; just sentient calm, just an ocean of tranquillity.

I have found these ideas in other people's dreams and in my own dream- then I learned about the dream of the cosmos. In spite of the vibrant realities in which all life, even the highest, may be endowed, the Supreme Ones I seek to bathe in, to encompass me and shelter me, know most of all how to dream. The pulses of the stars can touch our brains, revitalise our imaginations. For those whose dreams are centred, those who cravings will not be satisfied by earthly fulfilment, there is always the sharing...the uniting of the personal river with the original sea, at the point of knowing given to oneself; the personal focus on one's own aspect of the Dream. And, as a

woman, I would be honoured to share my life purpose within the Lady whose Essence is Life.
PH

BARD'S PRAYER TO BRIGHID

In half forgotten dreams I saw your face;
In thoughts enchanted could your beauty trace.
In years long past you knew the path I tread,
And thus I feel in some way you have lead
My intuitive sense to understand-
Begin the journey in your secret land.
Perhaps in some strange measure we are One;
When you, on Earth, Beloved of the Sun,
Still offer to the wanderers of this Age
The Wisdom of an ancient heritage.

The stars that seem to beckon modern man
Know well he understood when time began
More mysteries than he could hope to find
Within today's constrained and blunted mind.

Say, lady of those former times, whose links
With those of distant worlds, whose life-stream drinks
Of intertwining Oneness, help me feel
That in this lesser world we touch the Real;
That underlying everything we know,
Nothing has changed. As in the long ago
You dreamed my dream, so in humility
I find the trackway you reveal to me.
PH

Chapter Two

Ostara

OSTARA PRAYER
Risen sun of Springtime
Life which cannot die;
Keep us in Thy purpose
Constantly.
Energy of Sunlight
Stir our weary souls,
Give to us renewal
Totally.

Sad and disillusioned
In our thoughts we crave
For the reassuring
Touch of Truth.
In the flight for living
We reach out to seek the
Sun of Youth.

Humankind's Midwinter
Burdened us without
Knowledge of the Cosmic
Inner Light.
Sun of Earth's tomorrow,
Lead us from our sorrow
Out of Night.
PH

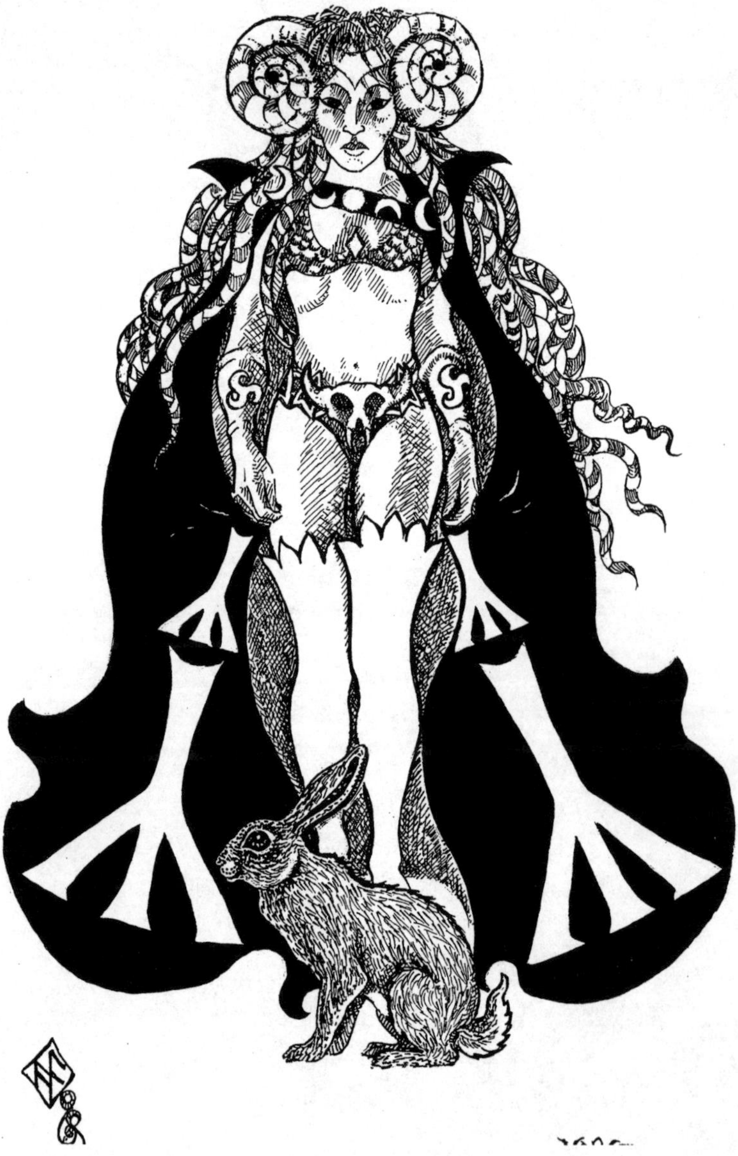

The Vernal Equinox

Ostara is celebrated at the vernal equinox and marks the real arrival of spring. It is a time of returning vegetation, the flowering of the gorse, daffodils, primrose and coltsfoot; sun coloured spring flowers. Animals and birds are nest building and mating.

We all know that Easter is often celebrated around this time. The name of the festival is derived from that of the Saxon Goddess Eostre, whose festival was celebrated in the spring. It was also the festival of the Phrygian Goddess Cybele, marking the death and resurrection of her son/lover Attis. Local Christians usurped the time to celebrate the death and resurrection of Jesus Christ.

Other Pagan themes run throughout the Easter celebrations- the Easter egg, visiting holy wells and springs and the Easter bunny, which is actually the sacred hare, the symbol of fertility returning to the land. The egg is the Pagan symbol of life and renewal. It is the 'World Egg' laid by the Goddess and split open by the sun God. The Hatching of the world egg was celebrated every spring. The original Easter egg was the serpent's egg, later replaced by a hen's egg, dyed red to represent the sun.

At the equinox the light and dark are in balance- day and night are of equal length, but the light is now gaining after the dark days of winter, towards the long days and short nights of summer, with their greater warmth.

The wheel of the year spins through time and the seasons, the sun, symbol of the Sky God, strengthens with the year.
AF

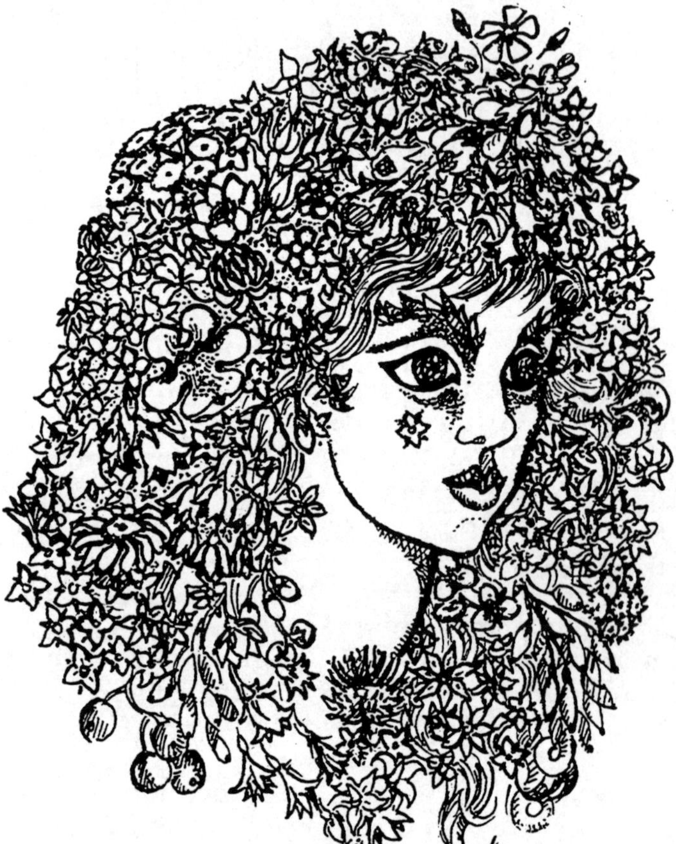

Gorse Tree Pathworking

Relax.

You find yourself on a hillside in the early spring. The sun is just rising. Around you you can see the gorse bushes just coming into flower and bright yellow daffodils nodding their heads in the gentle breeze.

All around you the earth is bursting into life with the coming of the strengthening sun and the spring.

Dew hangs on the sunshine yellow blossoms of the gorse and their heady scent fills the air, intoxicating. The humming sound of the first sleepy bees can be heard moving amongst the flowers as they drink the delicious nectar. You reach forward to pick a spray and the sharp spines prick you slightly, making you start.

As you do a disturbed hare leaps from its cover. You know that the hare is the sacred symbol of the Goddess and watch entranced as it gambols, unafraid of you.

Suddenly it stops, the air shimmers, and where the hare stood is now a beautiful young woman. Her hair is golden and dressed in a chaplet of flowers. She is wearing a long gown of green and yellow.

You walk towards Her and She looks up and smiles at you, so gleefully you feel your heart lift. She is the young Goddess of Spring. You may speak to Her if you wish.

She reaches beneath Her mantle and brings out a craved wooden goblet. It contains a yellow liquid made from the blossoms of the gorse flower. You take it from Her and drink.

It is like liquid sunshine coursing through your whole body, purifying and energising with the power of the sun and the earth turning to spring.

When you look again the Goddess has gone, and the hare is in Her place. You thank the hare and let the scene fade around you. Return yourself to waking consciousness.

AF

Flower Ritual

Now is the time to celebrate the coming of spring and the growth of the year. Decorate your circle or sacred space with as many flowers as possible. Make yourself a garland of flowers to wear in your hair. Have prepared a packet of flower seeds and a small flowerpot with compost in it, and a jug of water.

Cast the circle or bless your sacred space.

"I call upon the Goddess of the Spring, Blodeuwedd, the Flower Maiden. Honour us [me] with your presence here, tonight. I call upon you to witness this ritual. Fair Lady, listen to our words and be with us."

Meditate for a while on the coming of spring, the growth of vegetation and the birth of young animals. Think of how you would like to grow and develop during the year.

Take the seeds and place them in the pot:

"Goddess of the Spring, let me grow with the year, as these seeds grow. Let my spirit flower and grow beautiful. Let me recognise my times of growth and my times of retreat. Bless these seeds, Gentle Lady."

Water the seeds.

"Let your love and blessing be upon us all."

Share the cakes and wine. The rest of the evening can be spent in telling stories and poetry of the spring, making music and feasting. When all is done, close the circle.
AF

The Hare

Hares were sacred to the ancient British who associated them with moon deities and deities of the hunt. Killing and eating the hare was taboo. Until recent times the hare was not eaten in Kerry, as it was said to eat a hare was to eat your grandmother.

 The penalty for killing a hare was to be struck with cowardice. The Celts lifted the restriction on hunting the hare at Beltane, and made a ritual hunt and consumption. The Anglo-Saxons also venerated the hare and a ritual hare hunt was a feature of the spring festival of the goddess Eostre or Hretha. Folk survivals of these rituals still exist. The Hallaton Hare Pie Scramble still goes on in Leicestershire on Easter Monday. The men of the villages of Hallaton and Medbourne compete for bottles of ale. One large hare pie is made for the village to scramble over, though this is now dished out by the vicar. In former times an image of a hare was mounted on a pole and carried to the Hare Pie Bank before the games began.

Until the end of the 18th century an Easter Monday [originally Beltane] hare hunt took place in the Dane Hills, near Leicester, led by the mayor and corporation together with hunters and hounds. This hare was associated with Black Annis, a fearful hag said to live in a cave in the hills known as Black Annis's Bower, which she had gouged out of the hillside with her own claws. She may be the goddess Anu.

The patterns in the full moon are said to represent a hare, so the hare is associated with moon gods and goddesses. This hare in the moon imagery is appears in Chinese, Hottentot, Mexican, Indian and European tradition. There are many stories as to how the hare appeared in the moon. In Buddhist lore the Buddha was hungry and a hare sacrificed itself to feed him, leaping into the fire. In gratitude Buddha implanted its image onto the moon. The hare appears with the crescent moon in Buddhist and Hindu symbolism.

The Norse represented moon goddesses as being attended by a procession of hares bearing lanterns; Freya also had hare attendants. Celtic hunt and moon deities were associated with the hare and were often depicted holding them in their hands. For the Egyptians the hare was lunar, but also connected with the dawn.

In China the moon hare holds a pestle and mortar with which it mixes an elixir of immortality. Figures of white hares and rabbits were made for the celebration of the moon festival. It is a yin animal, a guardian of wild animals. It comes from the North Pole bringing the greetings of the moon goddess. In other Chinese writings a red hare appears with a phoenix and a unicorn, harbingers of peace and prosperity. Green jade hare amulets are made for good luck.

In North American Indian lore the Great Hare is the Hero/Saviour, Hero of the Dawn, father and guardian, creator and transformer. He is the Great Manitou who lives in the moon with his grandmother and is 'provider of all waters, master of winds and brother of the snow'. He is one of the well known tricksters, symbolising the quick mind which outwits physical force. The Algonquin Indians worshipped the Great Hare which was said to have formed the earth.

In Egypt the hare was depicted as greeting the dawn . The hare is associated with the east, dawn and Ostara. North American Indians described the hare god's residence as being in the east, sometimes on an island on a lake or sea. Thoth, Hermes and Mercury are also associated with the hare as messenger animals, as east is the station for light bringing gods. The risen Osiris is linked to the hare, so is the risen Christ as sun or vegetation deities.

The Teutonic goddess Eostre is often depicted as hare-headed. Her hare laid the egg of new life to herald the rebirth of the year. Even now the Easter bunny is said to distribute eggs in springtime. Eostre's name is preserved in 'Easter'. Easter, Ostara and Austre are cognate with the Sanskrit usra meaning 'dawn'. The old Norse austr means 'east' and gives us our modern word.

In Cambridgeshire a hare running through the streets is a sign that a fire is about to break out- the fire symbolism of the hare continues.

In Europe the hare is also associated with the corn spirit. In Anglo Saxon poetry the hare is addressed as 'the stag of the stubble, long-eared', 'the stag with leathery horns', 'the cat of the wood', 'the cat that lurks in the broom', the furze cat'. Hares hide in cornfields till the last reaping and the last sheaf is often called 'the hare' and its cutting called 'killing the hare', 'cutting the hare' or 'cutting the hare's tail off' .

The hare is associated with lusty sexuality and fertility. The hare is addressed in an Anglo Saxon poem as 'shagger'. It was sacred to the Greek goddess of love, Aphrodite, and her son Eros [and the Roman equivalents Venus and Cupid]. Philostratus said the most suitable sacrifice to Aphrodite was the hare as it possesses her gift of fertility in a superlative degree. The hare is quick, a prolific breeder even, as observed by Herodotus, conceiving while already pregnant. Hares genitals were carried to avert barrenness. Folk magic says that if anyone eats hare flesh for seven days it will make them beautiful. Pliny reported that people thought that if you ate a hare your body would be sexually attractive for nine days.

The hare is associated with madness, especially during the mating season when the animals may be seen boxing or leaping in the air and are said to resemble a coven of witches dancing. Like many animals sacred to the older religions, the Mediaeval Christians changed the hare into an animal of ill omen, saying witches shape shifted into hare form to suck cows dry. Stories abound of wounds inflicted on hares being found the next day on a woman. It was claimed that a witch in hare form could only be killed by a silver crucifix or bullet. The hare is the commonest witch familiar the world over. As late as the 19th century Brittany peasants would not speak of the animal and in Wales killing a hare was taboo. In the South West of England and in Kerry in Ireland peasants would not eat them.

The white hare is considered a ghostly or moon animal. This is not surprising as spirit hares do indeed appear with white auras. It was thought the appearance of a white hare was a death omen. A Cornish superstition says a young girl who dies after being abandoned by her lover will turn into a white hare to pursue her faithless love. In Christian lore the white hare, portrayed at the feet of the Virgin Mary, symbolises the triumph over passions. In Europe the white hare symbolises snow and the White Goddess of Winter.

The hare was used as a divinatory animal as young hares are born with their eyes open and never again close them, even to blink or sleep. Boudicca released a hare from beneath her cloak to predict the outcome of battles. Roman divined from its movements and its flesh was denied to ordinary mortals,
 In China the hare has powers of augury.

Much lore regarding the lucky or unlucky nature of the hare exists. Sailors considered hares so unlucky they could not be mentioned at sea. In some places a hare crossing the path was unlucky, especially for a pregnant woman who would miscarry or give birth to a child with a hare-lip. A hare's foot was carried as a charm to avert this, preferably from the left rear leg; losing the charm would prove very unfortunate. A hare's foot was said to avert rheumatism and cramps and help actors perform. The bone of a hare foot was carried as a good luck charm. Hare fat burned in a lamp was thought to make all present merry. Its brain was taken in wine before bed to prevent oversleeping. The genitals were used in aphrodisiac potions.

The hare is a sacred animal of the Goddess and is therefore a common witch familiar. It is a totem of the waxing year festivals of Ostara and Beltane, echoing the fertility of the earth and the power of the fire of the sun. It is a potent image of sexuality and sexual expression. The hare is touched by a divine madness, the anarchy which overturns dogmatic tradition and restrictions and brings new ideas and inspirations.
AF

OSTARA INVOCATION
Sun Lord of youth and beauty
Whose light is strong again,
The Earth sings thy praise,
The opening buds uncurl to warmth,
The leaves green the branches.

And in the equal dark
Strewn with a million diamonds
The moon reigns, calm, serene,
Arianrhod, whose radiance gleams
On earth, the Mother whose outstretched arms

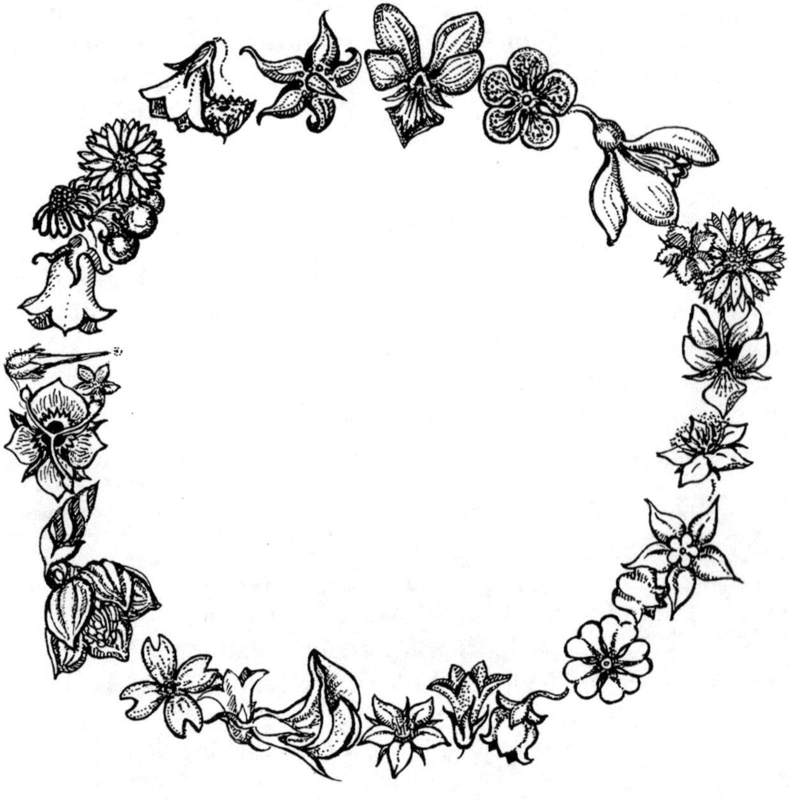

Nurture the children of a new year
And renew those who come from winter.
PH

Ostara Herb Craft

With Ostara comes the real arrival of spring. Fresh leaves green the trees, new vegetation covers the land and flowers are abundant. The Goddess hare shelters beneath the gorse, the tree totem of the vernal equinox.

The sacred foods of Ostara reflect the theme of the renewal of the Sun and Vegetation God and the beginning of the light half of the year. The common daisy [*Bellis perennis*] blossoms roughly from equinox to equinox and is sacred to the Celtic sun god Belenos. Tansy [*Tanacetum vulgare / Chrysanthemum vulgare*] celebrates the Sun Lord's renewal and is used in a traditional Easter pudding.

Some herbs are used to purify the body after winter to prepare it for the new life cycle of spring, such as tansy and gorse, the early flowering of which celebrates the renewal of the Spring Goddess. Cleavers [*Gallium aparine*] make a good spring tonic and ground ivy [*Glechoma hederacea / Nepeta glechoma*] in the ritual cup honours the Spring Goddess.

The underlying vernal equinox theme of the snake is very ancient, but persevered in folk customs and the popularity, at Easter, of bistort [*Polygonum bistorta*], also known as Snake Root, Easter Giant, Snakeweed, Dragon Wort, Easter Ledges and English Serpent Tree. The common name of bistort is derived from the Latin '*bis*' meaning 'twice' and '*torta*' meaning 'twisted'. This refers to the serpentine shape of the roots and accounts for many of its local names. Bistort was, and still is, traditionally eaten at Easter. In the north of Britain an annual contest is held to find the best Easter-ledge pudding.

Altar Decorations

Spring flowers such as daffodils, tulips and irises look beautiful on the Ostara altar. Make a sun wheel and paint it gold. Eggs should play some part in the decorations as the egg is symbolic of the rebirth of the year, the yellow yolk representing the Sun God and the white the Goddess, or the cosmic egg laid by the Goddess and split open by the Sun God. AF

SIMNEL CAKE
4 oz butter
4 oz brown sugar
5 oz plain flour
1 oz ground almonds
3 eggs
6 oz currants
4 oz raisins

Grated rind and juice of $\frac{1}{2}$ lemon
$\frac{1}{2}$ tsp. Mixed spice
$\frac{1}{2}$ tsp. baking powder
6 oz marzipan [almond paste]

Method
Cream the butter and sugar and gradually add the beaten eggs. Fold in the flour, almonds, spice and baking powder. Stir in the lemon juice and rind, and the dried fruits. Grease and line an 8" cake tin and spoon in half the mixture. Smooth down and put in a layer of rolled out marzipan. Add the rest of the cake mixture and bake at 180ºC/350ºF/gas mark 4 for 2 hours. Decorate the top with 13 marzipan balls.

This is a traditional Easter cake, the 13 decorations of the top supposedly representing Jesus and the twelve apostles, but actually a much older representation of the 13 lunar months of the year.

GORSE FLOWER TEA
4 tbs. gorse flowers
1 pint boiling water
Honey to taste
Method
Crush the flowers slightly and pour on the boiling water and infuse 10 minutes. Strain and sweeten to taste.

COLTSFOOT WINE
5 pints flowers
2 lb. sugar
1 gallon water
2 lemons
Yeast
Method
Pour three pints of boiling water over the flowers and squash with a spoon, cover. Leave 24 hours in a warm place, strain and add the lemon juice. Start the yeast, meanwhile boil the sugar in 3 pints of water and add to the flower juice. Cool to 20ºC and add the yeast. Cover and leave for 3 days and transfer to a demi-jon. Make up to 1 gallon with the remaining water. Fit an airlock.

This is one of the traditional ritual drinks of Ostara. Coltsfoot is sometimes called 'Son-afore-the-father' as the sunshine yellow flowers appear before the leaves.

GORSE WINE
1 gallon water
1 gallon gorse flowers
2 lb. sugar
1 lemon
3 oranges
1 cup of black tea
Yeast and nutrient

Method
Put the flowers in a jelly bag and drop it into the boiling water. Simmer for 15-20 minutes. Remove the bag, making sure you squeeze all the liquid out of it. Dissolve the sugar in the liquor and add the juice of the oranges and lemons and the grated rinds. Cool to lukewarm (20ºC) and pour into a brewing bin, add the tea, yeast and nutrient. Cover and keep in a warm place for 3 days, stirring daily. Strain into a demi-jon and fit an airlock.

NETTLE CHAMPAGNE
2 pints nettle tops
3 lb. sugar
1 lemon
Champagne yeast and nutrient
1 gallon water

Method
Peel the lemon, being careful to avoid the pith. Put the peel and juice of the lemon in a pan with the nettle tops and water. Simmer for 45 minutes and add the sugar, strain into a demi-jon. Cool to 20ºC and add the yeast and nutrient. Fit an airlock and leave to ferment out. Put in a cool place for a month and bring back into a warm place. Pour into strong, sparkling wine bottles and add a tsp. sugar to each bottle and cork tightly. Keep in a warm place for 7 days by which time a secondary fermentation should have started. Store in a cool place and treat bottles with care - do not shake or knock.

OSTARA INCENSE
1 part gorse flowers
3 parts frankincense
1 part benzoin
$1/2$ bluebell flowers
$1/2$ part bistort
1 part acacia
$1/2$ pine resin

Method
Blend together and burn on charcoal

EOSTRE INCENSE
1/2 part celandine flowers
1/2 part cinquefoil leaves and flowers
1/2 part orris root
1/2 part rose petals
3 parts frankincense
1 part benzoin
1/4 part dragon's blood
1/4 part nutmeg
1/2 part orange peel
Few drops frankincense oil
Method
Mix together and burn on charcoal.

The Serpent and the Egg

The symbolism of the snake is complex. It can be male and phallic or female, representing wisdom, in touch with the powers of the waters and the underworld, from which it emerges- a symbol of communication between the two worlds.

The healing aspect of the snake occurs in Celtic myth. It is associated with healing waters and the god Cernunnos, who is often shown holding a snake, or horned snake as a symbol of virility and fertility. As a vegetation god Cernunnos emerges from the underworld at this time to flourish and grow- symbolic of the shoot emerging from the seed below the earth.

The snake is also associated with fire, as witnessed by the ram headed serpent of Cernunnos and its association with Brighid. Bel is sometimes shown with a serpent or dragon, as are various other sun gods such as Apollo, Pythios and Helios. Amongst many peoples the snake was a sacred animal,

Serpents and the Egg

demonstrating the principle of life, death and rebirth as it sheds its skin and emerges renewed- symbolic of the earth renewed in spring after winter. It represents wholeness and its energy is that of creation, embodying sexuality, reproduction, psychic energy and immortality.

The egg is a universal symbol of life and creation, and so of resurrection. As a symbol of initiation it symbolises the twice born, its laying being one birth, its hatching another.

That the world is hatched from the cosmic egg is a pretty universal idea. In Hindu tradition the divine bird laid the cosmic egg on the primordial waters and from it sprang Brahma and the two halves formed heaven and earth. The cosmic tree is sometimes depicted as growing out of an egg floating on the waters of chaos.

In Egyptian legend the Nile Goose laid the cosmic egg from which Ra, the sun, sprang. In China the yolk was the sky and the white the earth.

The egg is closely associated with the serpent. One Egyptian legend says that Kneph, the serpent, produced the egg from his mouth. Orphism, holding the egg to be the mystery of life, creation and resurrection, often depicted the egg surrounded by Ouroboros, the circular serpent with its tail in its mouth. The Druids called the cosmic egg the egg of the serpent.

The egg is a prime symbol of Ostara and the rebirth of both the year and the Vegetation God. We use it to represent that rebirth, and also our own inner rebirth at this time of year, when the weather warms and our horizons become expanded- from our winter introversion and keeping close to the hearth, we go out and accomplish things. It is time to put to work the lessons we have learned from our winter reflections, deep inner visions and expansion of consciousness, and to bring that knowledge into the world. The egg reflects that potential, already once born, but waiting for its hatching. In the ritual the egg stands for our spiritual hopes in this yearly cycle.

DYED EGGS
Hen's eggs can be dyed using natural colourings:
Orange- boil the egg with onion skins
Pink- boil with beetroot and vinegar
Yellow- boil with turmeric
Blue- boil with red cabbage leaves and vinegar

The eggs can then be painted with sun wheels and other designs that are significant to you. If you want to keep the egg for a long time it should be blown first, or if you wish to eat it it should be hardboiled.

For vegans, eggs can be made from papier-maché [form with newspaper and wallpaper paste] then painted.

Drawing Down the Sun Ritual
This ritual should preferably be performed at dawn on the morning of the vernal equinox, though it can be performed during any other hour of the Ostara daylight.

The circle is cast as the dawn is breaking.

Priestess: *"This is the time of the balance of light and dark. The wheel turns towards the light and we embrace the light within ourselves."*

Priest: *"The Green Lord emerges from the winter cave, the underworld womb, into the light. The sap is rising, the earth is greening. The flowers blossom."*

He takes a glass vessel of water and the group wait in silent meditation for the sun to rise and illuminate the vessel and charge the water.

Priest: *"Lord of the sun, we call upon thee. Consort of the Goddess I call upon thee. Lord of the Green, I call upon thee. Charge this vessel with thy power."*

Priestess: [Taking the vessel from him] *"As we drink, let us embrace the light within us.* [She drinks and the vessel is passed around so that all may drink and each repeats her words. The priest drinks last and says: *Let each of us grow with the light."*

The circle is closed. If it is not possible to perform this ceremony, you can put out a glass vessel of water to be charged by the rising sun, and drink it as you awake.
AF

Rite For Ostara

The circle is decorated with yellow flowers such as daffodils, forsythia, tansy, coltsfoot, dandelions and so on. Boughs of greenery are also placed around. A bowl of seeds and a bowl of decorated eggs are placed on the altar. A candle is placed in the cauldron.

Indoors, we do not cast a circle, but simply bless the space.

Celebrant One:
"I call upon the Lord and Lady to witness that we come here tonight to celebrate the festival of spring, Ostara. I call upon the powers of the North, The East, The South and the West to guard and protect this place, which shall become for a time a place between places, at once a space for both the world of men and the world of spirit.

I invoke and call upon thee Fair Goddess of Spring, Lady of Flowers, thee I invoke. Descend I call to thee."

Celebrant Two:
"Mighty One, our Lord, all honour to thee, Consort of the Goddess, come I call thee. We are gathered here tonight to celebrate the festival of Ostara, when the Lord and the Lady meet as youth and maid. It is the festival of spring, when all about us life renews. The sun strengthens moving towards summer and his time of glory.."

Celebrant One: [Taking up the bowl of seeds]
"Hear ye, servants of the Lady and known that this is the time that the Goddess is renewed in all her glory. She is beauteous and young once more. Tall and graceful she walks amongst us as a maiden and our beloved one. Come our fairest Lady, grant blessing unto the seeds which become the flowers of tomorrow. Come O gracious Lady and protect that which is newly born, that children and animals grow strong beneath thy hands. Let the seeds be blessed in thy name O Goddess."

Celebrant Two:
"Come our gentle Lord, grant blessing unto the seeds which become the flowers of tomorrow. Come O gracious Lord and protect that which is newly born, that children and animals grow strong beneath thy hands. Let the seeds be blessed in thy name O Lord."

Celebrant One:
"Let the seed be cast to the earth. Let the fire of joy be lit which is the light of the growing sun and the light of the year."

The candle in the cauldron is lit in token of the equinox sun [if you are working outdoors, this is the signal for the bonfire to be lit]. The seeds are then gathered up and placed on one side to be divided up later amongst the celebrants.

The dish of eggs is then passed around and each person takes their egg. There follows a period of silent meditation on the season, the hopes that the egg represents or whatever message the Gods chose to send. Just wait for whatever comes. If you wish you could eat your egg to ritually absorb its message into yourself.

Celebrant One: [Taking up the cup of wine]
"Let the wine be blessed which is the wine of spring and the wine of the Queen."

[The wine is passed around the circle with a blessing.]

Celebrant Two: [Taking up the cakes]
"Let the cakes be blessed in the name of the God, our Lord."

The plate of cakes is passed around and each person eats.

When all work of the grove is completed the circle is broken:

Celebrant One:
"I call upon the Lord and Lady to witness that tonight we have celebrated the festival of spring, Ostara. Only they can know and measure our hearts. May they bless our hopes this night. It is not for us to bid them begone, but to ask that for all our days may they guide our paths. I thank the powers of the North, The East, The South and the West for guarding and protecting this place, which became for a time a place between places, at once a space for both the world of men and the world of spirit. Let the candles be put out, but let us remember the lessons of this night. The rite is over. Blessed Be."

All: *"Blessed Be."*
AF

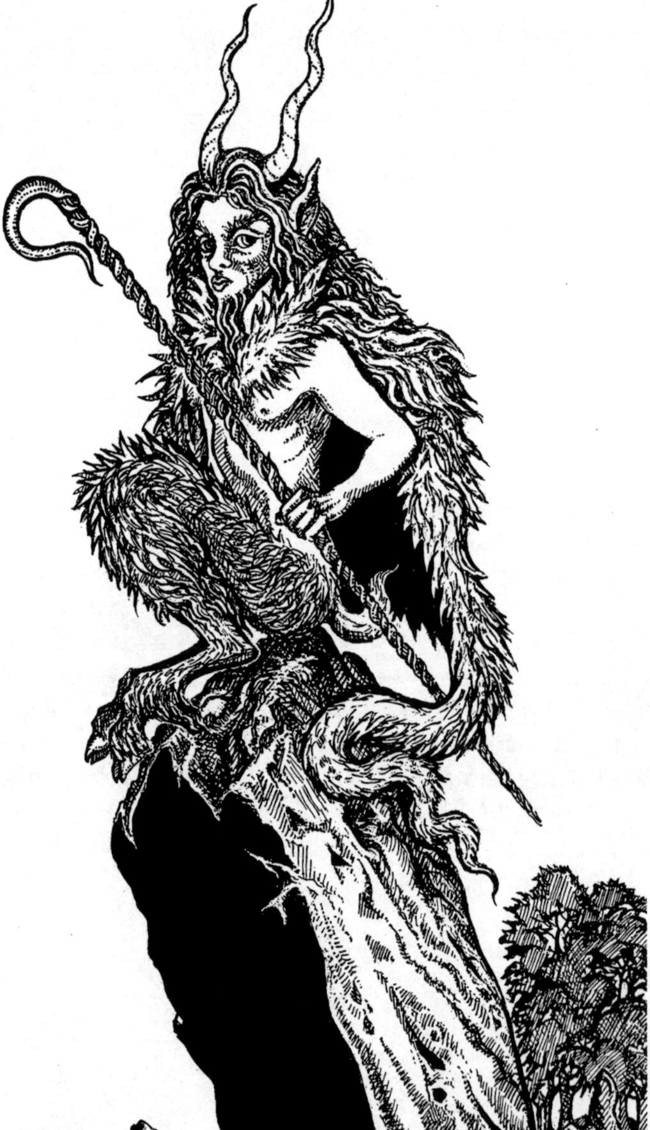

Chapter Three

Beltane

AVALON
From the fortress of Cunobelinus
On the slope of Dragon Hill,
They looked toward the Ridgeway,
And perhaps they look there still.

In the golden Celtic twilight
Of our fairy-haunted past,
Perhaps they still remind us
Of knowledge meant to last.

And their Avalon is there still,
Though our prosaic Age can't see
Through the veil of imperception
To the Lands of Mystery.
PH

The Coming of Summer

As the festival of Samhain marks the coming of winter, so Beltane is the real coming of summer, marked by the flowering of the hawthorn and the rising of the Pleiades. It is generally celebrated on Beltane Eve [30th April]. By now, the sun is in Taurus, the extended hours of daylight are very noticeable, and the weather is getting warmer. There is blossom on the fruit trees and the earth has greened over. Migrating birds such as cuckoos, nightingales and house martins arrive in Britain and begin to build their nests.

The word 'Beltane' means 'bright fire' and to the Celts was an early summer festival of fire, life and fertility. The name of Beltane is derived from the Celtic God Bel or Beli the 'bright one', God of light and fire, the Sky Father who impregnates the Earth Mother. Until recently fires were lit on hilltops on May Day to celebrate the return of summer. It was the custom to jump over the fire- young people to attract lovers, travellers to ensure a safe journey and pregnant women to ensure an easy birth. Cattle were driven through the ashes to ensure a good milk yield. The ashes were then scattered on the fields and the cattle were then taken to their summer pastures.

In many areas the May Queen is crowned with flowers, and she has a male counterpart in Jack-in-the-Green, or the Green Man. She represents flowers and new growth, he represents the death of winter and the rebirth of summer. She is covered in flowers, he is covered in ivy, holly, birch, poplar and fir greenery. They would have been appointed by the village as representations of the Goddess and the God and their performance reflected on the well being of the community; their coupling ensured fertility.

In some places the king and queen are still called 'the bride and groom'. Fertility would be ensured by all the villagers going off into the forest and performing sympathetic magic and any children of these 'greenwood marriages' would be named the son of the God, hence the surnames Robin-son, Hod-son etc.

The may pole is a phallic symbol of fertility and revelry. It is also the world tree or axis mundi, connecting the three realms. The magician uses the axis to climb to the Overworld or descend to the underworld. The dance around the maypole with some dancers circling sunwise, some widdershins suggests a dance of death and rebirth.

The Otherworld is very close at Beltane. Fairies could appear and they would carry off anyone falling asleep beneath hawthorn. Flowers picked in May have special magical properties.
AF

Beltane Herb Craft

The blossoming of the apple trees marks the return of the Summer Goddess, but perhaps the most significant herald of the season is the flowering of the hawthorn. It is said that the scent of the hawthorn is reminiscent of female sexuality, perhaps the sexual flowering of the Goddess. May Day used to be celebrated by people going off to the woods 'a maying' carrying back fresh branches and shoots. Magically, the hawthorn is a doorway to the Otherworld. Solitary hawthorns growing on hills or near wells were considered to be markers to the world of the fairies. Any human who slept beneath one, especially on May Eve, was in danger of being taken away to the land of the Sidhe. Hawthorn is so potently magical that it is forbidden to bring it indoors except at Beltane. It is wound about with the mysteries of the Goddess and should be treated with great care.

The dandelion is in full bloom, its golden flowers are very much associated with solar energies, bright life force and vitality. Dandelion leaf tea may be taken to enhance psychic powers and the flowers may be added to divination and sun incenses. The traditional time to make dandelion wine is St. George's Day, April 23rd. St. George may well be a Christian incarnation of a much earlier deity who overcame the dragon of winter and ushered in the summer around Beltane, while a twin deity would have brought in the winter.

Primrose is associated with the lusty currents of the season, growing life and fertility. The tea can be taken to attune yourself to the time of year.

Violets are associated with the twilight, a magical 'time between times', when the Otherworld is closer and it is easier to slip into, especially the turning of the wheel at Beltane. Violet wine or tea may be taken at twilight to facilitate passage into the Other Realms.

Sorrel [*Rumex acetosa*] and Common Mallow [*Malva sylvestris*] are both traditional food of love feasts, honouring the Goddess of Love and evoking the lusty currents of Beltane and its fertility aspects.

Honeysuckle is associated with cycles of change. The flowers twist around following the course of the sun during the day. It helps to connect with the cycles of change and the energy flow of each new season. It is also a herb of erotic love, the stems twine together like the embrace of two lovers.

Nettle is a herb of transformation; used at this time it marks the leaving behind of the winter and past painful experiences, and embracing the warmth of the coming summer. Catnip is a herb of friendship and love and may be used in a tea to cement those bonds at this time. Coriander is a powerful binding herb of love at this time, celebrating both the sacred love of the Lord and Lady and the love of human couples. Lady's Mantle is sacred to the Goddess and the feminine power of nature. It is used to contact the Goddess within.

PRIMROSE TEA
2 tsp. herb
½ pint boiling water
Method
Infuse 15 minutes. Strain.
Primrose is one of the sacred herbs of Beltane and the tea is taken to attune to the season, the growing currents of life and fertility.

HAWTHORN BLOSSOM WINE
2 quarts hawthorn blossom
1 cup black tea
3 $\frac{1}{2}$ lb. sugar
2 lemons
1 gallon water
Yeast and nutrient
Method
Grate the rinds from the lemons and boil them with the sugar for 30 minutes. Put the resulting liquid in a fermenting bin with the tea and cool to lukewarm. Add the yeast and nutrient. Leave 24 hours, stirring occasionally. Add the flowers, stand for 8 days, stirring daily. Strain into a demi-jon and fit an airlock.

MAY CUP
Handful woodruff flowers
1 pint cider
1 pint mead
Method
Place all the ingredients together in a jug and leave for 2 hours. Strain and serve.
This is an old British alternative to the German Mai Bowl.

BELTANE INCENSE
4 parts frankincense
$\frac{1}{2}$ part sorrel
1 part hawthorn flowers
$\frac{1}{2}$ part primrose flowers
$\frac{1}{2}$ part apple blossom
1 part oak bark
Method
Blend together and burn on charcoal.

LORD AND LADY INCENSE
1 part rose petals
1 part vervain
Few drops cinnamon oil
2 parts myrrh
3 parts frankincense
Method
Blend together and burn on charcoal.

AF

Rite For Beltane
The circle is decorated with boughs of flowering apple and hawthorn, primrose and honeysuckle and violet flowers. The altar is decorated with greenery- fresh branches, hawthorn blossom and early summer flowers. The candles and the cloth should also be green.

Priestess: "*We are gathered here tonight to celebrate the festival of Beltane, when the Lord and Lady celebrate their sacred marriage and the earth grows fruitful from their love. We come together tonight to give thanks for their blessings. Goddess, I call upon thee, in whose footsteps flowers grow. Thee I invoke come...come...come...*"

The Priest plunges the wooden spear or maypole into the earth.

Priest : "*Life to the earth!*"

The Priestess turns to him and exchanges his white cord (representing death and winter) for a red one (representing life and summer). "*To you, my beloved, I give life.*"

The Priest crowns her with a garland, for she is the May Queen "*To you, my beloved, I give beauty.*"

Priest : "*I bless the crops and the animals. I bless the seeds and the roots. I bless the stems and the buds. I bless the coming of life in plants, in animals and in children, in the name of* ... [God's name]."

Priestess : "*I bless the crops and the animals. I bless the seeds and the roots. I bless the stems and the buds. I bless the coming of life in plants, in animals and in children, in the name of* .... [Goddess name]"

They turn to each other and say "*God and Goddess, Blessed Be!*"

All : "*Blessed Be!*"

The cakes and wine are shared. Meditations, storytellings and handfastings may follow. There may be dancing around the maypole and the jumping of the Belfire. The High Priestess then blesses the cakes and wine which are shared amongst everyone. When all is finished the powers are thanked and the circle is broken. This is the signal for the feasting to begin.
AF

Contacting the Goddess Within

Prepare an infusion of hawthorn blossoms by putting $\frac{1}{2}$ oz of blossoms in a pot and pouring over 1 pint of boiling water. Infuse for 10 minutes and strain.

Go outside [if possible] to your garden or wild place early in the morning and set up a stone for an altar. Put the infusion in your cup on the altar and light two green candles. Decorate the altar with seasonal wild flowers.

Create your sacred space and put the tip of your knife into the cup saying:

"I bless this cup and ask that as I drink of it I may learn more of the wisdom of the Goddess who is manifest within me. I ask that I may learn more of her ancient ways and feel her love for all creation as my own."

When you are ready drink from the cup and feel the sacred flower spirit of the Summer Goddess contact your spirit within and become one with you. Gaze at the candle flames and the wild flowers and feel the earth blossoming and growing around you. Feel your spirit grow and blossom within you and become one with the current of the year, the manifest love of the Summer Goddess.

Pour the remaining liquid onto the earth as an offering to the Earth Goddess, saying

"White Queen, I thank you for being with me this day and ask that I may recognise that you are within me, as I dwell within you. Let me feel your presence in all things, visible and invisible. Let blessing be."

Close down your sacred space.
AF

Life on Earth

Mother Earth is the most fecund place in our Solar System. There is no doubt that Earth is the best place to be for us humans. But we share the world with a plethora of other life forms. From their point of view our presence here is not always an advantage. We are good at making ourselves uncomfortable with atmospheric pollutants and dumping toxins into the oceans; plants also breathe our air, and animals, fish, plankton live in our oceans. People are very aware of this situation now; we have all been educated in how to avoid the extinction of all life on earth. There has been a lot of talk and a certain amount has been done about it.

Folks who are Pagan or Green have notably been interested in the welfare of Mother Earth, but still millions out there live their lives, shrug their shoulders and hope fore the best. They want three cars per family, so what the hell? You can always stand on a hilltop and breathe, can't you? Perhaps when the human population has doubled, or trebled, you'll need to take your oxygen mask up there, just in case. Others take the view that the seas are big, so a little pollution doesn't count.

It isn't only our environment that comes in for neglect, or indifference, or worse. While Darwin insisted that man was just an animal, he [or she] is the most intelligent, the most worthy, of all creatures. Like everything else, this has yet to be proved. Animals and plants help to keep the Earth's balance. Birds and insects do work for us that we often do not recognise until they are no longer there. Humans have no special rights. Both humankind and animals have the right to love, life and freedom from fear and wanton cruelty, and not to fall victim to neglect or contempt.

As Celts, we recognise a Universe where all life is One. Where our Mother, the Earth, needs our protection more than ever before. Species of animals and plants are being lost forever. We cannot bathe in seas that are totally free from pollution. The air of our cities is still toxic, and forests that produce life-giving oxygen are still being eroded. This century has seen more loss of balance than any other time.

The chaos that has gripped civilisation is also reflected in thinking, the media, the all-grasping, undiscerning consumer society. But as individual we make up our own minds. We need not tolerate inhumanity to our fellow creatures, or look upon anything as merely a commodity. We ourselves are more than that too.

In the legendary Age of Chivalry personified by Arthur Pendragon our values would be seen as pathetic. There has been no time in history that lived up to the ideals of the legendary Logres, or the glories of the Tuatha de Danaan. But in the Arthurian myths these values are expressed and encoded in chivalry, the feminine appreciated, and not just in the sexual sense.

Poets in the Celtic age were the Aos Dana, the gifted people. The present age gives little encouragement to enlightened imagination, whether expressed in poetry or prose. The subject matter of all life is interrelated. At last it may be possible to reclaim for the whole design its former beauty, renew in the Sea of Life the promise of Manannan, and give to Earthly dawning intelligence the illumination of Lugh, and the quiet splendour of Arianrhod.

In this, our Island sanctuary, we alone make or destroy the peace- and what if we are weighed in the Cosmic balance and found wanting?
PH

The Sacred Animals of Beltane

The two great Celtic festivals of Beltane and Samhain centred around the needs of cows. At Beltane cows were taken up to their summer pastures, after being driven through the ashes of the Bel fire to purify and protect them. At Samhain, they were brought down to sheltered winter feeding grounds. At Beltane, in Scotland, came the spilling of the caudle on the ground, a milk offering for protect of the herds. The cow is the avatar of many mother goddesses symbolising the power to give birth, to protect, love feed and nurture. The cow often represents Mother Earth while the bull represents the fertilising Sky God, providing everything needed for Her children - soil to grow things, food to eat, plants to heal and teach.

SACRED ANIMALS OF BELTANE

The cuckoo is a summer visitor to Britain. When you first hear the cuckoo, whatever you are doing you are fated to do for the rest of the year. The cuckoo is the bird of the Otherworld Tir-nan-Og. Cuckoo is said to go to the mysterious realm of the land of the dead in winter, entering the fairy mounds.

The king stag was a beast with twelve or fourteen points on his horns, and a stag would have to have been seven years old to have twelve points. The Taliesin poem states " I am a stag of seven tines", seven points on each horn. The seven tines represent the seven lunar months from Samhain to Beltane. The roebuck acquires his new red coloured coat at Beltane.

The Abbot's Bromley Horn dance was originally a Beltane ritual, later transferred to September, and the character of Red Robin Hood appears at it. Robin Hood may once have been a stag god, or Lord of the Forest.

The Pleiades [in the constellation of Taurus], which rise at Beltane, were also known as 'the Doves', the sacred birds of Venus/Aphrodite. Doves are emblems of faithfulness as they pair for life; a pair of doves was a traditional wedding gift. Doves were associated with all queens of heaven and mother goddesses, symbolising the soul or breath that was derived from the Mother.

In Norse myth an eagle sits at the top of Yggdrasil, the World Tree, representing summit of spiritual achievement. It is at war with the serpent at the tree's roots. As a solar power the eagle is in conflict with the powers of the Underworld and winter, represented by the snake. Some species of eagle eat serpents and can sometimes be seen carrying them. It is an expression of the tension between the sky and the Underworld, between summer and winter, between light and darkness. The eagle was thought to renew itself by flying to the sun and scorching its feathers before plunging into the sea to emerge as a young bird. It is a symbol of the resurrection of the spirit, renewal and the power of life over death.

For the Greeks and Romans the goat represented virility. Goats are fertile and reputedly lusty, so have a prominent significance in nature based religions. Some goddesses and their priestesses are pictured as riding upon them. The Greek god of the wild Pan was the son of Amalthea ['goat']. Pan and his Satyrs had the legs, horns and beards of goats. In the Swedish May play Bukkerwise the goat god [or his priest] was mated with the goddess, sacrificed and resurrected, a fertility ritual connected with the revival of the vegetation spirit.

Hares were sacred to the ancient British who associated them with moon deities and deities of the hunt. Killing and eating the hare was taboo. Until the end of the 18th century an Easter Monday [originally Beltane] hare hunt took place in the Dane Hills near Leicester led by the mayor and corporation together with hunters and hounds. This hare was associated with Black Annis, a fearful hag said to live in a cave in the hills known as Black Annis's Bower, which she had gouged out of the hillside with her own claws. She is possibly a winter/crone goddess figure, who gives up her powers at Beltane. The hare is associated with lusty sexuality and fertility, addressed in an Anglo Saxon poem as 'shagger'. It was sacred to the Greek goddess of love, Aphrodite, and her son Eros. The hare is quick, a prolific breeder even, as observed by Herodotus, conceiving while already pregnant. It is a totem of the waxing year festivals of Ostara and Beltane, echoing the fertility of the earth and the power of the fire of the sun. It is a potent image of sexuality and sexual expression. The hare is touched by a divine madness, the anarchy which overturns dogmatic tradition and restrictions and brings new ideas and inspirations.

On May Eve in Minehead the town's hobby horse appears. For the next three days it prances around the town accompanied by a flute and accordion. On May 1st the Padstow 'Obby 'Oss appears. Villagers say May Day is more important to them than Christmas. The evening before, the village is decorated with green branches and flowers. The sinister black 'Oss, led by the teaser parades through the town to the accompaniment of drum and accordion. Now and then the drum falls silent, and the 'Oss gradually falls to the floor, only to rise again. At midnight the 'Oss dies, only to be reborn at the next summer.

In Greece a May Day ceremony was held on Mount Pelion. An old man in a black sheep skin was 'killed' and brought back to life again by his companions, dressed in white sheep skins. Presumably this represents the death of winter and the coming of summer in a pantomime similar to that of the May Day hobby horses in Britain.

In England, at Holne near Dartmoor, a May morning ram roast took place. A ram was roasted whole in its fleece and a scramble took place for pieces of it. The ram is an emblem of solar powers. The horned god Cernunnos is depicted as holding a ram-headed serpent. The serpent is the waning year and the Underworld powers, while the ram is the waxing year and the horns connect to the solar/sky powers.
AF

Chapter Four

Coamhain

COAMHAIN HYMN
The Wheel turns, full Summer Light
Spreads from horizon to horizon.
The shortest night fades into rosy Dawn.
The zephyrs fan the golden days.
Flower clad Earth rejoices.
Winter a far-off memory,
But the Wheel turns,
And fruits need to ripen,
And the Earth needs some calm
Before the energy of another Spring.
But now at Midsummer all Nature sings
Like the birds, of the triumph
That they will always know again and again.
PH

The Golden Season

The Summer Solstice, which we call Coamhain and which the Druids call Alban Heruin, is an important festivals in the Pagan calendar. It falls around the 21st June. By the summer solstice there are only six hours of darkness, but eighteen hours of daylight. It is the zenith of the sun in its yearly cycle. Therefore the festival celebrates the strength of the Sun God at the height of his powers.

·THE COMING OF SUMMER·

From this time, though the days will grow hotter for a while, they also will grow steadily shorter until the time of the winter solstice, when there are six hours of daylight and eighteen of darkness.

Folk customs suggest that this pivotal point in the year continued to be celebrated down the centuries with bonfires and festivities. The building of Midsummer fires continued into the nineteenth century, particularly in Orkney and Shetland where seals were believed to shed their skins and dance through the night. In some places the tradition of Midsummer fires has been revived. On June 23rd in Carn Brae the first bonfire in a chain across Cornwall is lit. The chain extends from Lands End through to Sennen, Sancread Beacon, Carn Galver and St Agnes Beacon to the Tamar. Each bonfire is blessed by the local clergyman in Cornish, herbs and wild flowers are burnt. Young people leap across the embers to drive away evil and to bring good luck.. At St Cleer the fire is crowned with a broomstick and a sickle with a newly cut oak handle is thrown onto the flames to ensure the fertility of crops and men.Midsummer has always had a reputation as a time for magic and divination, or as a time when the sidhe and spirits are abroad, not just in Britain, but all over Europe. Any number of folk customs bear this out. Young girls would use the magic of the season to divine their future husbands. Other, less pleasant secrets could also be learned: it is said that if you stand in the churchyard on this night a vision of all those who will die this year will pass before your eyes.

In the Craft the solar year is often seen as being ruled over by two opposing kings- the Oak King, lord of the waxing year, and the Holly King, lord of the waning year. At each solstice they battle for the honour of ruling. At the close of the summer solstice the Holly King begins his rule, which is relinquished at the winter solstice to the Oak King. This idea of two gods, one of summer or light, and one of winter or darkness appeared in many cultures. Apollo was viewed as having slain the python at Delphi with his sun ray arrows The snake may be seen as the Lord of the Waning Year, and the dark twin of the Sun Lord. The two lords fight for rulership of the land at the beginning of summer, and at the beginning of winter. Ra, as the solar cat, was seen as battling the serpent of darkness Zet or Set. Similar stories are told in many myth systems of sky gods fighting serpents, such as Marduk and Tiamat, Zeus and Typhon, Yahweh and Leviathan etc. This may have given rise to the later debased myths of the hero slaying the dragon [instead of defeating him for the summer months] as in the story of St. George and the dragon. In the Pagan world view the slain lord will rise again every year, and the light and dark [winter and summer, day and night] rule in balance. Later myths see death as a final ending and the light and dark are in opposition.

On a personal level, Coamhain is time to celebrate achievements, to acknowledge your own talents and power acting in the outer world. It is a time for fun and joy, for enjoying the light and warmth.

Coamhain Herb Craft

Certain plants were said to have strange properties at the time of the summer solstice, for example, an elder cut on Midsummer Eve would bleed real blood, or fern seeds could confer the gift of invisibility if gathered at midnight on Midsummer Eve. Today witches believe that plants gathered at the time of the summer solstice are imbued with special magical properties, charged with the power of the sun's zenith. There are a number of plants which are particularly associated with midsummer, and which were gathered by the old herbalists and wise women at this time.

St John's Wort would be gathered on the Eve and made into garlands to wear or hang inside the barn. The golden flowers are associated with the sun and the flames of the Midsummer fires; an old name for St. John's wort was amber. It was believed to possess the quality of protecting the wearer against all manner of evil, and that the plant moved around to hide from its pilferers. Legend has it that if a young woman should pick St John's wort on the morning of Midsummer Eve with the dew still fresh upon it, she will marry within a year.

Angelica corresponds to the direction of the south and the element of purifying fire, the quarter of the Summer Solstice, noonday and Magical Will. Angelica is one of the sacred plants of Coamhain and ritually invokes the power and healing energy of the sun.

Bay is also infused with the power and energy of the sun, and may be used to invoke the Sun Lord and his gifts of divination, healing and protection, especially at the Summer Solstice, when it should be gathered for magical purposes.

Marigold or calendula flowers represent the sun and its passage through the wheel of the year. The dried petals can be used in incenses. Dried or fresh the petals can be used to make a ritual tea or wine for the solstice.

Fennel was held in high esteem by the Romans and was one of the nine sacred herbs of the Anglo-Saxons. During the Middle Ages fennel was hung over the door on midsummer's eve as it was believed to keep away evil spirits. It is one of the sacred aromatic herbs of midsummer, used as an incense or thrown on the bonfire.

Nothing visually evokes the warm summer sun as much as the giant yellow-faced sunflower, which moves during the day to follow the path of the sun across the sky. Magically it represents strength, courage and action. The petals may be dried and use in incenses during sun rituals or during meditations and exercises designed to increase your confidence and self image or to determine a course of positive action. For the solstice feast the seeds can be eaten raw or added to bread, cakes and salads, or used as a coffee substitute.

The primary power plant of the summer solstice is the oak. In ogham the oak is 'duir' meaning 'door' in Gaelic. The word for door and oak, and perhaps Druid, come from the same root in many European languages. The oak flowers at midsummer and marks the door opening on one side to the waxing and on the other to the waning year. When the oak flowered the druids made an infusion from the flower buds as an internal cleanser for the body, and washed in water found in the hollows of oak as a ritual cleanser for the midsummer rites.

It is at this time that the mistletoe berry turns golden. Those found growing on the sacred oak was especially prized, as the soul of the oak was believed to be present in the mistletoe.

COMFREY FRITTERS
1 egg white
2 oz cornflour
2 tbs. water
Young comfrey leaves
Method
Beat the egg white until it forms stiff peaks. Blend the cornflour with the water until it forms a smooth cream and fold it into the egg white. Dip the leaves in this batter and deep fry until golden.

Comfrey is common in the British Isles and can be found growing in damp places such as ditches, by rivers and streams. It flowers from June to October. Comfrey is a herb of protection and healing; its value is particularly potent at midsummer.

AINE'S DELIGHT
6 heads of meadowsweet flowers
2 egg whites
$\frac{1}{4}$ lb. cornflour
Water
Sugar
Method
Mix the cornflour with a little cold water to form a thin paste. In a separate bowl, whisk the egg whites until fairly stiff. Add a little sugar and continue to whisk for a further minute. Carefully fold the egg whites into the cornflour paste to make a light frothy batter. Dip the flower heads into this batter and fry them until golden brown. Whilst still hot, roll the fritters in sugar and serve immediately.

CLARY SAGE TEA
1 oz herb
1 pint boiling water
Method
Infuse for 15 minutes and strain, adding a little sugar or honey to taste.

Clary sage is a herb of divination, and the dawn watch of midsummer is a powerful time for seeing into the other realms.

BLACK MEAD
4 lb. blackcurrants
2 lb. honey
$\frac{1}{2}$ pint red grape concentrate
$\frac{1}{4}$ oz malic acid
1 gallon water
Yeast and nutrient
Method
Mash the blackcurrants and put them in a brewing bin. Boil the water and add the honey to it, stirring to dissolve. Pour over this the blackcurrants and cool to 20°C add the yeast and

nutrient and stand for 3 days in a warm place, stirring daily. Add the concentrate and malic acid and strain into a demi-jon and fit an airlock.

ELDERFLOWER WINE
1 pint elderflowers [without stalks]
2 lb. raisins
Juice of 1 lemon
³/₄ lb. sugar
1 gallon hot water
Yeast and nutrient
Method
Place the flowers in a brewing bin with the hot water. Stir, pressing the petals against the sides of the bin. Wash and chop the raisins and add, together with the lemon juice. Stir well and cool to 20ºC. Add the yeast and nutrient. Cover and keep in a warm place for 10 days. Strain into a demi-jon. Stir in the sugar. Fit an airlock and leave to ferment out.

HEATHER ALE
2 pints of heather shoots
1 lb. sugar
Yeast
1 lb. malt
2 gallons of water
Method
Put the heather in a pan, cover with water and boil for 15 minutes. Strain into a brewing bin and add the sugar and malt. Stir to dissolve. Add the rest of the water and cool to 20ºC. Add the activated yeast and cover. Stand for 5 days and bottle into screw top bottles. Ready to drink after 7 days.

The Picts brewed a legendary ale from heather, the recipe for which was a secret. Invading Norsemen tortured the guardians of the secret to obtain the recipe to no avail. Heather is a sacred plant of midsummer and represents the spirit of the vegetation God.

COAMHAIN INCENSE
4 parts frankincense
2 parts red sandalwood
1 part heather flowers
½ part mint
½ calendula
½ part fennel
½ part angelica
½ part St. John's wort
½ part camomile
Method
Blend together all of the ingredients and burn on charcoal.

Coamhain Ritual

The altar should be decorated with golds and yellows- this theme is echoed through the candles, cloths and flowers, which might include the traditional summer herbs of St. John's wort, fennel, marigold, camomile, chervil and marjoram. Centrally placed should be a sun wheel or sun representation.

The circle may be decorated with gold and shining sun symbols. Herbs can be placed about it such as fennel, marjoram, camomile, lavender, St. John's wort and yarrow. Ritual robes or clothes are yellow and gold. The bonfire, if you have one, should contain oakwood. If not, a yellow or gold candle can be placed in the centre of the circle in the cauldron.

This ritual is for a minimum or four celebrants, two of which take on the role of Oak King and Holly King. Women can take on these roles if there are not enough men present. They should prepare wreaths of oak and holly respectively. The other celebrants can wear chaplets of the sacred Coamhain herbs and flowers. If there are only three of you, one person can do the roles of both celebrants, or if there are only two of you, the parts of the Oak and Holly Kings can be omitted, and the final speech of the Holly King given to one of the other celebrants.

Cast the circle.

Celebrant one: "*Lord of heaven and power of the sun, we invoke thee in thy secret name of ...[God name], O Lord of the greatest light. Now is the time of thy glory and power. Place your shield between us and all power of darkness. Shoot forth your arrows of light to protect us. Grant to us at this time green fields and good hunting. Give to us orchards of fullness and corn that has risen high. Show us within the time of Splendour, the pathway to the peace of the Lord and Lady.*"

Celebrant two: [plunges her wand into the cauldron] "*The knife to the cup, the rod to the cauldron, the sun to the earth but the flesh to the spirit.*"

Celebrant one: "*Now is the time of the sun when our Lord ... [God name] is at his height in the heavens. Yet it must also be remembered that now is also the time of ...'s* [God name] *decline to his death and rebirth at the darkest time of winter.*"

Celebrant two: [Crowning the Oak King with his wreath] "*I crown you the Oak King, lord of the waxing year. Now is the time of your greatest power. Are you ready to do battle?*"

Oak king: "*I am.*"

Celebrant two: [Crowning the Holly King with his wreath] "*I crown you the Holly King, lord of the waning year. Your season is almost upon us. Are you ready to do battle?*"

Holly king: "*I am.*"

There follows a choreographed battle between the Holly and Oak Kings, at the end of which the Oak King falls to the floor.

If there is not sufficient room for such a battle to take place, a symbolic passing of a sceptre or similar can be substituted.

Celebrant two: *"Holly King, lord of the waning year, I name you the victor. Now is the time you take up the sceptre and rule the land of the Goddess until the time of the winter solstice, when once again you will do battle with your brother."*

Holly king: *"As it is with the God, so it is with man. We also journey throughout our time, from birth until death and to rebirth upon our way. We must remember that the Goddess will raise the God with the kiss of rebirth and send him, yet again, upon his journey. We also go down to the cloak of her darkness and her veil hides us from mortal sight. But the tomb is the womb of time from which we return to other lives, to share once more the knowledge and love of our fellows and friends."*

Everyone sits down around the fire and the vigil begins to await the dawn. Now is the time to share the Coamhain brew, engage in divination, feast and cast incense in the fire.

When the dawn breaks dissolve the circle, and taking a light from the fire go to wherever you can to watch the sun come up. It is encouraged with chanting and drumming and traditionally the firing of flaming reed arrows into the sky.

Oak Tree Pathworking

The primary power plant of the summer solstice is the oak, the king of the forest, huge, living for centuries. In Britain there are reputed to be oaks which have been standing for a thousand years. The roots of the oak are said to extend as far underground as its branches do above, making a perfect symbol for a god whose powers royally extend to the heavens, middle earth and the underworld equally. It is a symbol of the law "as above, so below". In ogham the oak is 'duir' meaning

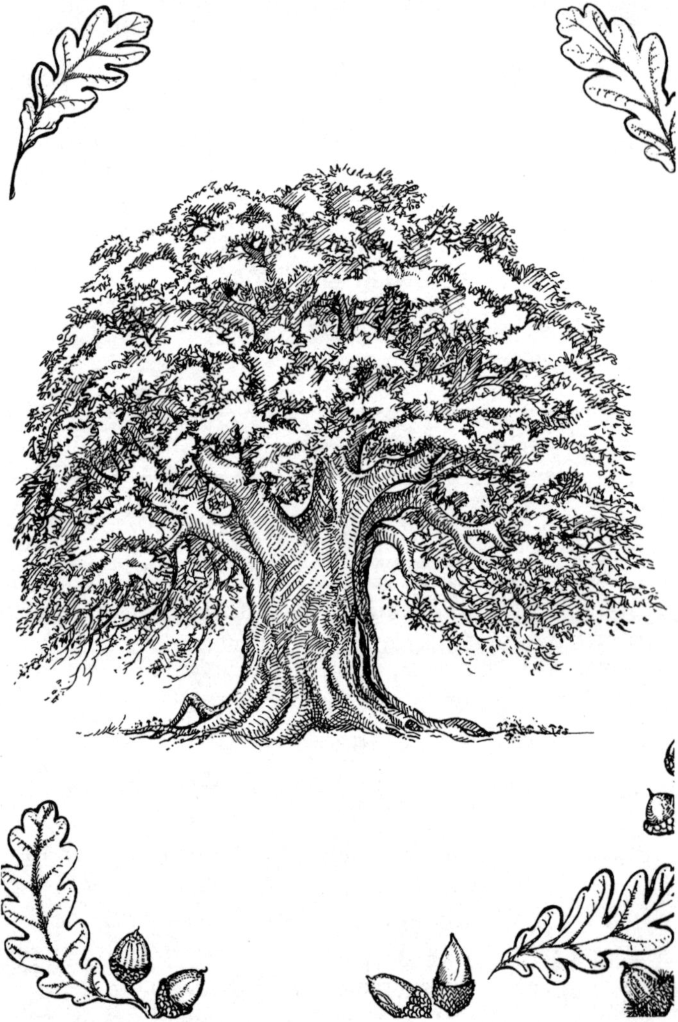

'door' in Gaelic (the word for door and oak, and perhaps Druid, come from the same root in many European languages), perhaps because a door made form oak offers protection and solidity and because oaks often marked boundaries; or perhaps because the oak is the door to knowledge and marks boundaries of a different kind.

The oak flowers at midsummer and marks the door opening on one side to the waxing and on the other to the waning moon. It stands at the turning of the year. When the oak flowered the druids made an infusion from the flower buds as an internal cleanser for the body, and washed in water found in the hollows of oak as a ritual cleanser for the midsummer rites

Relax.

It is Midsummer Eve. You find yourself in an ancient forest, alive with the power of magic. In the star studded sky you can make out the Corona Borealis, the Spiral Castle of Arianrhod, lingering on the horizon.

Following a pathway, you come to a clearing. In the centre stands a huge oak tree. It is the king of the forest, enormous, centuries old. The branches spread as a canopy above, while you know that its roots extend as far below ground.

It is a magical axis mundi, linking all the three realms of existence.

The oak is hollow, and you squeeze yourself inside a natural doorway into the warm trunk. You can see out both sides.

The oak stands at the boundary of the year, between the time of the waxing sun and the time of the waning sun.

As you look out from where you entered you can see the past. Look out from the other side and you can see the future. You can feel the year turning.

You easily climb up the hollow trunk into the canopy of branches.

The solstice sun is rising on the longest day. You greet the sun at this time of its greatest strength and power.

Feel its strength absorbed into your own body as the rays of the sun warm you. You feel your life turning towards a new cycle with the turning of the year.

When you are ready thank the oak tree and return yourself to waking consciousness.
AF

MIDSUMMER HYMN
Above me shone the stars
Before the dark clouds came;
Could I believe that my star
Was so powerful, so near?

On imagination's wings
I reached the edge of space;
Below me was the web of lace
That shield from sunlight clear.

Too clear for me to know,
To really understand
But nearer to the Earth again
The Sun could take my hand.

I feel warmth upon my face,
And know it is a true embrace

That yields within the cloudy wreath
The touch of Life instead of Death.
PH

The Journey That Never Ends

I first passed near Stonehenge in my uncle's car on the way to Devon from London. I was a refugee, a World War Two evacuee. I was little more than a baby and I did not see the stones. If I had, I am sure I would never have forgotten them. Their haunting majesty would have imprinted on my mind.

The forest of tree-rock, some say erected by magic, has viewed the triumph and tragedy of humankind for millennia, its eternal circle speaking silently of a union it seemed then in 1939, and often now, that the world would never achieve. And in that war torn world it was hard to believe in magic and subtlety, or Gods who could influence the paths or mortal destiny.

Britain was then basically Christian, but in the aftermath of war this began to fall apart for many people, especially the young in a metropolis like London. By the time I was a teenager education and personal questioning led me to have doubts. A perception from early childhood had never entirely left my consciousness: I had only briefly believed in fairies, but I had seen them depicted in tales for children often based on distorted recollections of past centuries where such beliefs were discouraged by the church. Strange, humanlike but not human, with a beauty and personality beyond the mundane. Some were gods and goddesses; some drawn from the Greek and Mediterranean pantheons, some Celtic. I did not forget.

The temple of modern thought is based on materialism, a faceless edifice. The temples of our ancestors were erected to honour mystery, the hidden worlds of nature, without which humanity is driftwood on the sands of time. The circles of stone show Oneness, everlasting completeness- and an understanding of it. Life is a series of patterns where the Present Moment is the actual, the real within the Real. The Ridgeway paths lead to a West where two worlds might more easily interact; the realm of Tir Nan Og, which blends with everywhere and needs no journey to reach, but which modern eyes and dulled minds cannot easily perceive..

In the freedom of intuitive imagination we are able to rediscover our place in Nature. Perhaps the jigsaw puzzle of existence will show clearer delineation, and parts that are mean to come together can be sensed. Many of our hopes 'civilisation' has torn apart. It was not constructed Forever; unlike the stone circles it does not seek to manifest the Eternal. But our life is part of the Everlasting Cycle, and perhaps in the coming years it will show itself- as flowers grow in cracks in dusty pavements.

Then we can withstand the storm of ignorance, with Angus Og be allowed through the 'siege of fairies'. Perhaps it is he who is poetically referred to as 'the Dreamer whose Dream came true'. The primal ocean of Manannan touches the shores of the Celtic lands, and our hopes and dreams can become tomorrow's reality. Like Manannan, we spring from Lir, the boundless All, where nothing moves - and we make the journey that never ends.

MIDSUMMER INVOCATION
The Evening Star glows- in the forest
Leaves quiver, the Summer wind sighs,
Looks for the vanishing Springtime,
The dream that, once known, never dies.

The memories held in moonlight
Enrap me in love's subtle power,
Reflecting the Promise Eternal
That shapes a leaf, touches a flower.

It's midsummer now, and the young moon
Sheds everywhere a warm glamourie,
The stars hold the fire of Midsummer;
Again they have brought you to me.

Enfold me within this enchantment,
Regain in the stillness our joy,
The Gods have returned to us the verdure
That no Winter cold can destroy.

The trees of the forest climb slowly-
Reach out for the sunlight afar;
Untaught- their roots tap the immortal-
The Earth that was born of a Star.
PH

The Bee - Avatar of the Summer Goddess

The Great Goddess is often pictured as a queen bee. Cybele was seen as the Queen Bee for whom her priests castrated themselves to become her drones [as the drone is emasculated by the Queen during mating]; they were called the melissae, the 'bees', as were the priestesses of Demeter. The officiates at the mysteries of Eleusis were also called 'bees'. The Greek for bee melissa gave its name to lemon balm or *Melissa officinalis* which, according to Pliny, attracts bees above all other plants.

Another favourite food of bees is heather. At midsummer Cybele, as Queen Bee, imprisoned Attis in heather. Osiris was also imprisoned in heather, freed by Isis, presumably also as

Queen Bee. The Roman love goddess Venus courted Anchises on the mountainside to the hum of bees. The Greeks consecrated bees to the moon.

A very old belief states that bees were born in the body of dead animals, particularly the lion and the ox [this appears in the Bible in the story of Samson], so they were seen as symbols of rebirth: new life coming from death, or perhaps even the soul of the animal taking the form of bees. In Greek myth Aristaeus killed a lion on Mount Pelion and from the wound emerged the first swarm of bees.

Even now you find bees carved on tombstones. In Egypt the bee was giver of life and therefore immortality. It denoted royalty and was emblem of the Pharaoh of Lower Egypt. A Breton story says bees sprang from the tears of Christ on the cross, another slain and risen god.

Christian tradition says bees originated in paradise and they are called 'the little servants [or messengers] of God' so is unlucky to kill one. In the Mithraic cult it was associated with souls as a psychopomp. Greeks believed that the souls of the departed could enter bees. With their special knowledge of souls, bees were sometimes seen as prophets of death; it was an omen of forthcoming demise when bees swarmed around a house or on a dead tree.

They were considered wise creatures with special knowledge of the future. They are meant to know all the old lore. A Scottish saying goes 'ask the wild bee for what the Druids knew'. The Celts believed they held secret wisdom which they derived from the Underworld.

Bees are associated with divine inspiration. They were the 'birds of the muses', bestowers of eloquence and honeyed words. Virgil called bees the 'breath of life'. Plato was called 'the Athenian Bee'; as a baby a swarm of bees alighted on his mouth. This story is also told of other poets and orators including St. Ambrose and Xenophon. Sophocles was called 'the Attic Bee' from the sweetness of his words. It was once believed that bees were self-fertilising, therefore they were associated with chastity and virginity. The Romans believed that bee keepers should be celibate. Tradition has it that bees will not sting a virgin.

Bees are symbolic of hard work and early monastic orders were based on the structure of the hive, symbol of good government and industry. Christianity associated bees with diligence, order, prudence, chaste virgins and the Virgin Mary. A busy hive represented the ordered life of a religious community. The bee is the Christian and the hive the church. Islam associates bees with the faithful, and with intelligence and wisdom.

A 'bee' is a social gathering for some useful work, such as an apple-bee, a husking-bee and so on. It is an old Devonshire custom that was exported to America in the Elizabethan era.

Honey was the usual sweetener before the introduction of sugar, and mead was very popular. Beeswax was used for the best candles. Some say that bee stings cure rheumatism.

Because of their special powers and associations, more lore has grown up around the keeping of bees. Bee keepers should tell all the family secrets and news to a hive, especially a death in the family, repeating three times 'Little brownies, little brownies, your master [or whoever] is dead'. If this is not done the bees will die or fly away. A bride must inform them of her marriage or they will leave the hive. A piece of wedding or funeral cake should be left for the bees:

A Maiden in her glory,
Upon her wedding -day,
Must tell her Bees the story,
Or else they'll fly away.
Fly away-die away-
Dwindle down and leave you!
But if you don't deceive your Bees,
Your Bees will not deceive you.

Marriage, birth and buryin',
News across the seas,
All you're sad or merry in,
You must tell the Bees.
Tell 'em coming in an' out,
Where the Fanners fan,
'Cause the Bees are justabout
As curious as a man!
Rudyard Kipling

The hive or swarm should never be moved without first telling the bees why. Bees should never be sold, but a gift of bees gives good luck to both the giver and receiver. Honeysuckle or melissa rubbed on the hive will ensure the bees will never leave. They should not be moved on Good Friday or they will die. In Wales it is said that if a bee flies round a sleeping child that child will have a happy life. A swarm of bees denoted misfortune, while possession of a headless bee averted the evil eye. Apache Indians believe that some bees kept in a box will afford good luck and protection.

In Hindu lore the bee on the lotus symbolises Vishnu, while blue bees on the forehead symbolise Krishna. Bees also representing the combined sweetness and pain of love when they appear on the bowstring of the Love God Kama.

Bees are highly organised creatures, always busy and highly productive. They always know exactly where they are going-we still have the phrase a 'bee-line' for the shortest distance between two points or for going straight to something. Bees work for the good of their community rather than for themselves alone.

The honey bee was seen to orientate itself on its journey by the angle and position of the sun, and the Celts regarded it as a messenger who travelled the paths of sunlight to the realm of the spirits. Being winged they share with birds the ability to carry messages from this world to the world of spirits and the practice of telling the bees news means sending messengers to souls in the Otherworld.

Bee Pathworking

Relax.

You find yourself in a summer meadow, standing before a dome shaped straw hut. The sunshine is bright and warm and the meadow is full of flowers, you can smell their scent. A gentle breeze is blowing and you can hear birdsong and the gentle hum of bees going from flower to flower to drink the nectar.

You enter the hut and find yourself in a six sided room, the walls a warm, pale yellow. Shafts of sunlight come in through the slatted roof. In the centre of the room a woman sits. She has long, blond hair and is clothed in a golden robe, edged in black. Several young women wait on her, dressed in yellow and speaking in low murmurs, like the hum of bees.

The Lady smiles at you and beckons you forward. She hands you a golden cup and you drink from it; a sweet honey brew of mead. The warmth of it courses through you and you know that it is a brew of inspiration. Take some time to feel what inspiration it brings. If you wish to you may speak to the Lady and ask her for answers to your questions.

When you are ready, thank the Queen and leave the chamber. Let the scene fade around you and bring yourself to waking consciousness.

Chapter Five

Lughnasa

LUGHNASA PRAYER
Rippling beneath a summer wind
The golden stalks of corn
Bow down their heavy heads of seed
To earliest Autumn dawn.
The offering to the Summer Lord
The firstfruits of the year
A golden anchor, silken cord
That binds the Goddess near.

And we, who need our daily bread
That we may still survive
Can offer in our secret hearts
The hopes by which we live.
May he to whom my life is pledged
Grant me His life and power
And She, who rules to Earth's far edge
Bless this, our harvest hour.
PH

Season of Summer Ripeness

Lughnasa is celebrated on the nearest full moon to 31st July. It marks the start of the grain harvest and in the Middle Ages was celebrated with a loaf made from the first harvest called hlafmaesse ['loaf-mass'] from which we get the more modern name of the festival 'Lammas'.

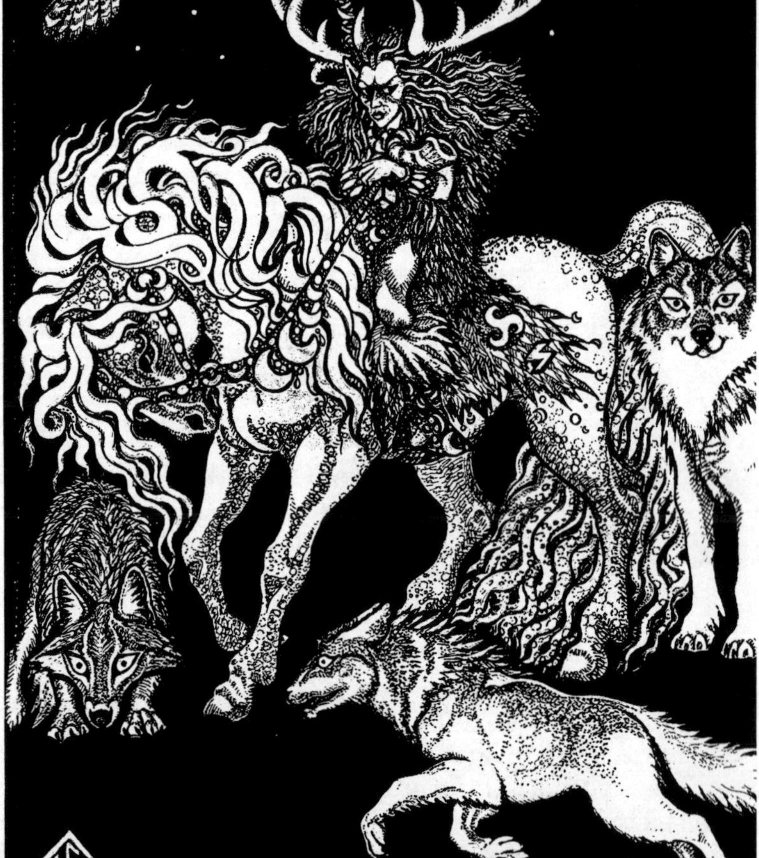

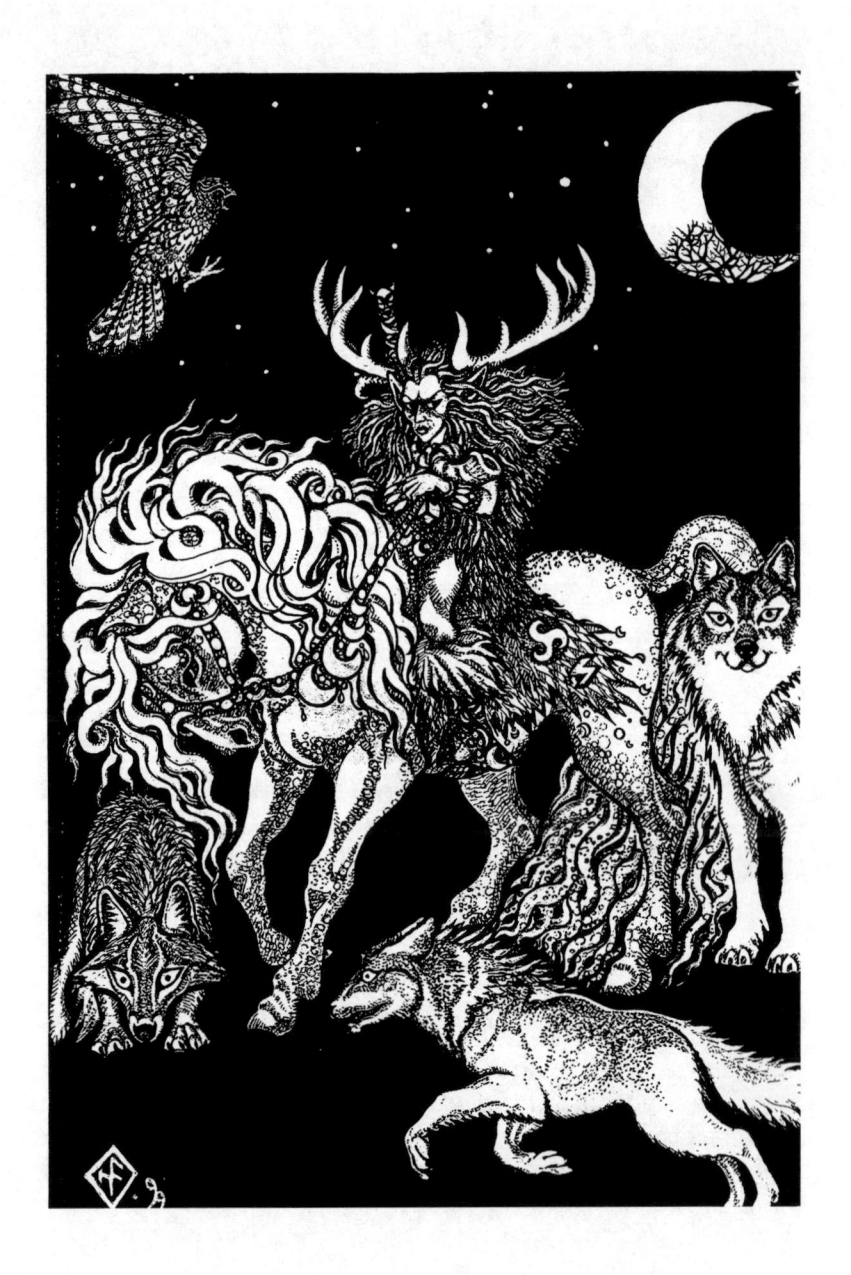

Lugh was a Celtic fire God who spared the life of his enemy Bres in return for knowledge of agriculture. He mated with the sovereign Goddess of the land and underwent a ritual death and rebirth.

At Lughnasa the Celtic tribes would gather for competitions and games. The festival lasted for two weeks and it was prophesied that as long as the tradition was upheld there would be 'corn and milk in every house, peace and fine weather for the feast'.

In the Craft we celebrate the festival of the God and man at Lughnasa, as a counterpoint to the festival of the Goddess and women at Imbolc. It is the beginning of the harvest and the celebration of the God as Corn Lord before his decline and death at Herfest. The men set up the circle and hold rough games, perform hunting magic and honour the God.
AF

The Stag

The stag was one of the four sacred animals of the Celts and has played an important part in folklore in many areas of the world. The earliest representations of the stag god, or of the shaman dressed in stag horns, date from round 12000 BC, the most famous being the 'sorcerer' of Les Trois Freres. Stags appear on Old Stone Age Paintings and carvings. Antlers have been found buried at Newgrange and sites in Glastonbury and at Stonehenge. The stag was sacred to the Great Goddess in the bronze age. A guild of deer priests called 'the Fair Lucky Harps' had their headquarters at Donegal.

Stags clean their new antlers in august and September, rubbing off the velvety coating on the branches of trees. and the rutting season begins from then on, often going on into November, driven to greater ferocity by the frosts. Perhaps for this reason the stag is associated with the Otherworld, and

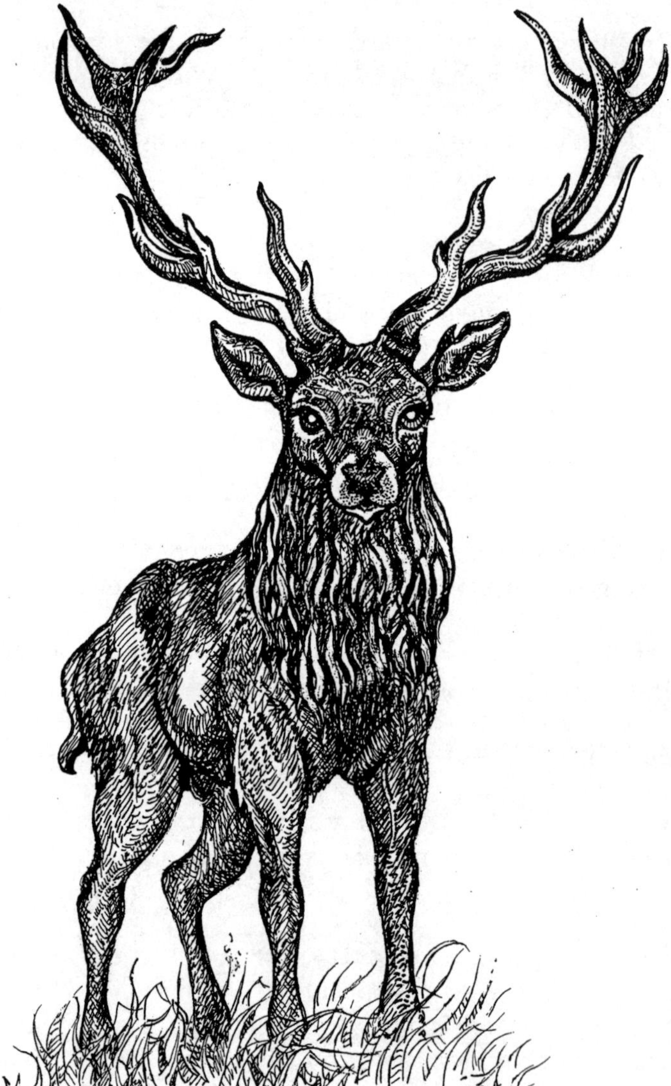

rules over winter the festival of Samhain and the midwinter solstice. During the winter, the stag herds are said to be protected by the Cailleach or Hag Goddess and her women, who herd and milk them.

In Arthurian legend, the knights would take part in a yearly hunt of the white stag, and its head would be presented to the fairest lady in the land. This is probably a seasonal tale of the battle between summer and winter. It was once thought that the 'King Stag', leader of the herd, should be ritually hunted and killed every year to ensure the return of summer. The white stag may be seen as a solar symbol. Legends often tell of a stag fighting with a snake, or underworld/winter animal, sometimes drawing it from the ground with its nostrils and then swallowing it or trampling on it.

The stag is most closely associated with the Gaulish god Cernunnos, who wears stag horns. He is portrayed on the Gundestrup cauldron, dating from 300 BC as a seated figure with antlers growing from his head. He holds a snake in one hand and a torc in the other, showing that he is a god of winter and summer, sky and underworld, death and resurrection. He is surrounded by the animals of the forest. A secondary illustration shows him as Lord of the Animals, holding aloft a stag in either hand. Cernunnos was an intermediary between the animal kingdom and man, a guardian of the gateway to the Otherworld. The stag is rarely portrayed in Celtic art except with the stag god.

Remnants of the ancient stag cult may be seen in the legend of Herne the Hunter, possibly a British stag god equivalent to the Gaulish Cernunnos. Herne the Hunter is said to still haunt Windsor Great Park and to ride out with the Wild Hunt at the midwinter solstice. He is described as a mighty, bearded figure with a huge pair of stags horns on his head. He wears chains, carries a hunting horn and rides out on a black horse with a pack of ferocious hunting hounds.

Stags, especially white ones, frequently appear in myth as Otherworldly animals, who entice heroes to the Otherworld or herald their deaths. Pwyll, Prince of Dyfed, while out hunting, chanced to meet Arawn, Lord of the Underworld hunting a stag, and became temporarily Lord of the Underworld himself. The stag Arawn was hunting was Pwyll's soul. Oisin was the son of the deer goddess Sadb and near the end of his life saw a vision in which a hornless fawn was pursued over the waters of the sea by the red and white hounds of the Underworld. The fawn was himself. Llew saw a stag baited to death and was soon afterwards murdered by his wife Blodeuwedd's lover, Gronw.

In some countries the image of the unicorn supplanted the mysterious white hart as the herald of otherworldly events, though not in Britain, Mediaeval romances continued to feature the beast. Richard II adopted a 'white hart lodged' as his personal emblem, and it still appears on many pub signs. St. Hubert, patron saint of huntsmen is said to have chased a white stag through a forest for many weeks before it appeared to him with a cross between its antlers.

The king or royal stag was a beast with twelve or fourteen points on his horns, and a stag would have to have been seven years old to have twelve points. The Taliesin poem states " I am a stag of seven tines", seven points on each horn. The seven tines represent the seven lunar months from the winter solstice to the summer solstice or perhaps from Samhain to Beltane. As the stag was considered to be a sacred royal beast, its hunting was often the preserve of the nobles, perhaps originally only the priest-king.

The roebuck acquires his new red coloured coat at Beltane. The Abbot's Bromley Horn dance was originally a Beltane ritual, later transferred to September, and the character of Red Robin Hood appears at it. Robin Hood may once have been a stag god, or Lord of the Forest.

Horned beasts were generally considered sacred, the horns a symbol of fertility. Antlers were amongst the earliest tools used to till the soil, and powdered stag antlers are among the best fertilisers known to man. In North America antlered deer dancers performed to increase fertility by causing rain and encourage the growth of wild crops. The genitals were frequently used in love potions. The gall of a deer mixed with honey caused conception when anointed on the genitals. The musk sac filled with milk and herbs was a protection against danger and bad luck, brought fortune in sports, games, war, cured insanity and unconsciousness.

The stag is an important symbolic animal, though it rarely appears in Celtic art, except in the company of the Horned God. Cernunnos bears the horns of a stag which connect him to the Upperworld, the fertility of the earth and the Underworld.

In many myths a mysterious white hart appears to the hero, challenging him to hunt it through the forest. It may lead the hero into the Otherworld. The stag turns out to be his own soul, and the hunt a necessary lesson. What does the spiritual hunter hunt? He hunts his own true Self. The fate of the antlered king, like the white stag symbolised the soul growth that required radical changes on all levels of consciousness.
AF

Stag Pathworking
Relax.

You find yourself in a deep forest walking along the animal tracks through the undergrowth. The tree canopy is very thick, and little light gets through. Through a gap in the trees you catch sight of a white stag grazing. It is a beautiful beast with branching antlers, each bearing seven points. You know that this is a magical animal and watch in awe.

Suddenly, the stag seems to sense your presence and with a quick movement lifts its head. Its eyes look straight into yours for a moment before it starts and begins to run from you, deeper into the forest. You realise that this is a challenge for you to follow, and to keep up if you can.

As you run through the forest you see various animals that with an inspired insight, you know are aspects of yourself. Always, the stag remains a little ahead of you.

Eventually, you come to a clearing, and the stag is standing in the centre of it. You are panting and breathless, but the stag seems unaffected. It is waiting for you and you go forward to meet it. It seems to invite you to touch it, to embrace it.

As you do you melt into each other and you know that the stag is the higher aspect of yourself that you have been seeking. On your brow you have antlers which branch upwards and connect you with the higher powers. Your coat glows white and pure and you realise what you can be.

You begin to run through the forest with new power, you have the strength and senses of the stag. You can see and sense much more. You feel full of energy, and have a sense of great freedom, you glory in your own strength and swiftness. You can go wherever you will.

After a while you come to a stream and pause to drink. The water is fresh and pure. You see your stag reflection. You walk into the stream to bathe and it washes over you.

As you wade back to the bank you find that you are walking on your own two feet and helping yourself up with your own two hands. The horns on your brow have gone, but you can still feel where they have been. The strength and the power of the stag seems to remain with you.

Thank the stag. Allow the scene to fade around you and bring yourself back to waking consciousness.
AF

The Warrior

The weapons of the psychic warrior are his body, mind and spirit. These must be trained to work in harmony. The warrior faces his own fears, he develops his spiritual courage, hones his Will. Will is not impulse or desire, it is the unwavering strength that seeks the personal truth and path.

There are many methods that seek to harmonise the mind, body and spirit- yoga, the martial arts etc. It may help to pursue one of these for at least a time, to learn how the mind affects the body, how the body affects the spirit and so on.

We are all subject to many fears, and it is the warrior's purpose to seek them out and defeat them. It must be recognised that the body has its own fears, fear of injury, fear of physical danger. These are natural and proper. Without these fears we would put our hands in the fire, crash our cars, jump off cliffs. The body has an inbuilt mechanism of self preservation. I didn't fully realise this until I had a near death experience a few years ago; my mind and my spirit were quite willing to depart from the body, calm and resigned, but my body, quite independently, was panicking. It clings to life, that's its job. The warrior may decide to face many of his physical fears to develop his will and courage- to get on an aeroplane when he is afraid of flying for example. Fear facilitates a change in consciousness, to conquer a fear facilitates the development of the Will. To do something so dangerous that it may result in injury or death, however, is no part of the warrior's path it is self-indulgence.

The warrior may subject himself to physical extremes to force his will and consciousness beyond the ordinary. Religious sects around the world have subjected neophytes to extended fasting, heat, cold, isolation etc. My personal view is that these methods simply weaken the candidate, and make them more susceptible to indoctrination. They are the techniques of brainwashing. If anybody tries to do this to you, run a mile! Your spirituality is your own quest, and you must find your own truth. You can do much more than you imagine, break your self imposed limits. Anyone who has ever taken part in fire walking will realise just how far the mind and the will can overcome what you think is possible.

The deepest fears lie within the mind itself, they arise from childhood and adult experiences and conditioning. Such fears limit us, and prevent our development. At some point the warrior must confront them, one by one, and deal with them. The strength of the warrior is won through trial and experience and is never boasted about or used to inflate his or her own ego. The warrior has honour, and treats others with equal consideration. The warrior is at peace with himself or herself- strength does not come from building walls which suppress all feeling.

The warrior follows his or her path boldly, wherever it leads.
AF

Lughnasa Herb Craft

This is the time of summer ripeness, with an abundance of fresh produce including tomatoes, cucumbers, onions, baby carrots, broccoli, cabbage, beetroot, cauliflowers, fresh salad, courgettes, beans and peppers. Lughnasa is also the start of the apple and grape harvest, and there are ripe fruits such as peaches, apricots, gooseberries and plums. The special ritual foods of Lughnasa are apple, basil, borage, chicory, fenugreek, fennel, honeysuckle, poppy seeds, grapes, vine leaves and nasturtium flowers, as well as wine, beer and bread.

Basil [*Ocimum basilicum*], also known as Sweet Basil and the Witches' Herb, falls under the dominion of the planet Mars. It is a herb that is said to impart courage and immortality through death. Basil may be used at the festival of Lughnasa, when the Lord, in his prime prepares for death at Herfest. The combatants of the Lughnasa games may eat basil to fortify their courage.

Borage [*Borago officinalis*] is associated with warrior gods. It was one of the magical herbs of the Celts. The common name may be derived from the Celtic word 'borrach' meaning 'person of strong courage or bravery'. Our Celtic ancestors would steep borage leaves in wine and the mixture would result in a very significant rise in the blood adrenaline level. To give courage to the Crusaders borage was added to stirrup cups drunk at their departure. It is believed that carrying borage flowers can bring you courage. Borage can be used to an aid of psychic powers and to stimulate courage and strength. It is particularly useful when exploring the warrior path. Borage tea or wine may also be taken at Lughnasa if the traditional chases and battles are to be undertaken. A strong infusion can be drunk to aid psychic awareness, and can be used in the ritual bath in preparation for inner journeying, vision quests and shamanic practices of an arduous nature. Borage tea and wine can be taken at the feast to make merry, and bring gladness to the hearts of the participants.

Chicory [*Cichorium intybus*] is associated with the God as Corn Lord, and this is the time when the grain harvest begins in earnest. The flowers open from early morning to noon only, and will not stay out any longer, even on the sunniest day. The flowering of the chicory marks the period of the harvest, beginning in July at Lughnasa and ending at the autumn equinox. The fleeting nature of the flowers reminds us of the transient nature of time and the seasons.

Fenugreek [*Trigonella foenum-graecum*] is associated with Sun Gods and is used at the Lughnasa ritual to honour the waning sun.

The grape vine [*Vitis vinafera*] is closely associated with the sun. Its name is derived from 'viere' meaning 'to twist', referring to its spiral growth. Far from being introduced into Britain only at the time of the Romans, the vine was well known and propagated before the bronze age. The Danaan people were said to have taken the vine with them when they invaded Ireland. The use of wine in magical ceremonies is well known, as it changes the consciousness of its imbibers, releasing inhibitions and perhaps allowing instincts greater reign, sometimes even releasing prophetic powers. Intoxication was once seen as divine state, allowing worshippers to be possessed by their god. The grape harvest begins at Lughnasa, when we celebrate the powers of the Sun God who has ripened the crops. Vines and grapes may form the decorations and the garlands at Lughnasa, and of course may be drunk! It is also charged as 'the blood of the earth pressed smooth', reminding us of our reliance on the body of the Goddess for our food and drink, our very lives.

The apple harvest also begins at Lughnasa, the time of strength and fruitfulness, when the God prepares himself for his decline and death at Herfest. He is honoured with Lamb's wool or Lammas wool (from the Gaelic La Mas Nbhal or 'feast of the apple gathering'), a hot spiced drink of cider and ale, with toast or pieces of apple floating in it. Each person takes out a piece and wishes good luck to everyone, before eating it and passing the cup on.

PLAITED LUGHNASA LOAF
$1 \frac{1}{2}$ tbs. sugar
$\frac{1}{2}$ oz yeast
6 fl oz milk
1 lb. plain strong flour

Pinch salt
3 eggs, beaten
for glaze:
1 egg beaten
Poppy seeds
Method
Start the yeast with a little sugar and the slightly warmed milk. Sift the flour and salt into a bowl. When the yeast is frothy add it to the bowl with the eggs and sugar. Mix to a smooth dough. Cover and leave in a warm place for an hour to double in size. Knead until smooth, divide into three strands and plait together. Place on a baking tray, cover and leave to prove for another 40 minutes. Brush with egg and sprinkle on the poppy seeds. Bake at 220ºC/425ºF/gas mark 7 for 15 minutes. Reduce the temperature to 190ºC/375ºF/gas mark 5 and bake for another 25 minutes.

BORAGE TEA
2 tsp. dried herb
1 cup boiling water
Method
Infuse for 10 minutes, strain.

BORAGE WINE
2 pt. borage flowers and leaves
1 lb. raisins
2 lb. sugar
Juice and grated peel of one lemon
1 cup black tea
Yeast
Method
Wash and chop the flowers and leaves. Put into 5 pints of water and bring to the boil. Simmer for 5 minutes, remove from the heat and leave to infuse for 24 hours. Bring $1\frac{1}{2}$ pints of water to the boil and add the sugar, stirring until dissolved. Strain the infused mixture into a fermentation bin and add the sugar mixture. When cool add the raisins, tea,

juice and grated peel of lemon and the yeast. Cover and leave for a week, stirring daily. Strain into a demi-jon and top up with cold boiled water. Fit an airlock and leave to ferment out. When fermentation is completed rack into a clean demi-jon and leave to clear.

YARROW WINE
1 gallon boiling water
4 lb. white sugar
1 oz yeast
1 slice toast
3 quarts yarrow flowers
Rind and juice of 4 lemons

Method
Pour the water over the flowers and soak for 5 days. Strain the liquid into a pan with the sugar and orange rind. Simmer for 20 minutes. Slice the rest of the oranges into a brewing bin and pour the liquid over. When cooled to lukewarm [20°C] spread the yeast on the toast and float on top of the liquid. Ferment for 14 days, then strain into a demi-jon and fit an airlock.

LUGHNASA INCENSE
2 parts benzoin
1 part oak wood
$1/2$ part gorse flowers
$1/2$ part basil
$1/2$ part borage
2 parts frankincense
A few drops of pine oil

Method
Blend together and burn on charcoal.

HORNED GOD INCENSE

½ part oak moss

1 part benzoin
1 part pine resin
2 parts crushed juniper berries
Few drops cedar oil
Method
Mix together and burn on charcoal.

LUGH INCENSE
3 parts frankincense
1 part oak bark

½ part mistletoe

1 part heather flowers
Method
Mix together and burn on charcoal.
AF

Rite For Lughnasa
By Lughnasa the hours of daylight have noticeably begun to decline. It is the time of the 'first harvest' and the Corn Lord is called upon to face his sacrifice for the good of the people. It is marked with feasting and funeral games. In the traditional Craft it is the festival of men and the God.

The men proceed to the circle and set it up. It is decorated with alder boughs, borage, yarrow, vine leaves, and pine needles. The fire is lit with alder and pine. The men work up male energy by running through the woods, painting their bodies and donning animal masks. The High Priest invokes the God and hunting magic is performed. Trials of strength and prowess are undertaken. The men are then reminded that the women are waiting and may or may not be invited to enter.

High Priest : "*This is the festival of man, the hunt and the harvest which provides for the time of darkness. Yet the God stands alone without his proper consort. She must grieve for his departure and take him to the dark places. The women have been excluded on this night. How say you, servants of ...* [God name]*, shall we let them enter?*"

If the men decide against the women entering, they must close the ritual of their own accord, but the women are usually called in to witness that the Lord will die but his death gives us the strength to carry life. The women are reminded that this is the time of the God and men and if they enter they must enter as warriors and join in the rough games. If the women are permitted to enter they will be taught some secret hunting magic etc. and be reminded that the God's death is in itself a promise of rebirth. This is the time for silent commune with the God.

Drumming and chanting follow and the test of worthiness follows, whatever the group decides this should be, some game or contest of strength and skill. The victorious contestant then stands on the Stone of Destiny and swears an oath of fealty to the Goddess and to the land and his brothers and sisters of the Craft. He then becomes the Sacred King until Herfest and marked with spirals of woad, which will last until Herfest. The cakes and wine are shared. Feasting and stories of Gods and heroes follow. The circle is then closed.
AF

REALISATION
I wander through the valley of my youth;
The summer breeze yet whispers of my dreams.
The quivering leaves still speak of ancient truth
That time-defies all Mankind's devious schemes.
In outward terms my life had lost its path,

And now my footsteps falter in their track;
Where is my home, my sure abode, my hearth?
My mind alone can search the journey back.

Are we not One, whom these sad years divide?
Can Earthly nature all our hopes enshrine?
In this enchanted vale you walk beside
This ageing woman, whose eyes seek some sign
In things apparent and illusion-born,
Cities of man and their abundant yield,
Of flowers hidden in the ripening corn
That fruits on Earth and in Elysian field.

Can I believe the harvest to be so near?
The secret dedication of my life-
The streamlet's muddied waters will run clear
And smiling Nature recognise my strife.
We are but threads entwined in the Design
Of all that will be, and has been before.

Enough that I am yours and you are mine;
We will gather yet from the golden store.
And all the frost that smote our early days
And froze a but that had no chance to bloom,
Will melt as with my trembling lips I praise
The Gods whose dreams may stir within my womb.
PH

Blessing the Grain Ritual

You will need a sheaf of corn or a corn dolly. Set up your sacred space then invoke the Goddess:

Priestess: *"Golden Goddess, whose hair is the waving yellow corn, crowned with poppies. Golden Goddess, whose glorious harvest feeds us. Descend I beseech thee and give blessing to thy children"*.

"She takes up the corn:
Fields bright with corn,
Drenched with sun.
Lughnasa, beginning of the harvest.
The Mother, the Maiden are One.
In Hellenic garb Demeter and Persephone,
Or Brighid in all the Celtic lands,
Or Isis who watches over the fertilising Nile;
The Mother gives us bread, life-
Her arms seek to shelter us
Even in this age when we
Find it hard to see her face
In the dust of the modern world;
The technical jungle
Whose human seeds
May yet reunite us with the stars.
Where the Gods have always lived,
And from where they will come again-
As now, in glimpses in the woodland and plain,
Or where the seeing eye can look beyond
The dimness of the mind, the fettered logic
That never dares to dream, and find order again
In the pattern of Time and Space.*"

Priest: [Taking the corn] "*I am the plant of life, which comes forth from the God, which grows from the ribs of the God, which allows people to live, which makes the gods divine, which spiritualises the spirits, which sustains the masters of wealth and the masters of substance, which enlivens the limbs of the living. I live as corn, the life of the living, I live upon the God of the Earth, but the love of me is in the sky, on earth, on the water and in the fields. Now the Goddess is content, she rejoices for her son. I am life appearing from the God.*"

Now follows a period of meditation and communing with the spirits of the earth.

Afterwards the cakes and wine are shared. Songs and poems to the harvest are sung and there is feasting in the fields.

When all is done the circle is closed.

AF [* Lughnasa hymn by PH]

La Mas Nbhal

The apple harvest also begins at Lughnasa, the time of strength and fruitfulness, when the God prepares himself for his decline and death at Herfest. He is honoured with Lamb's wool or Lammas wool (from the Gaelic *La Mas Nbhal* or 'feast of the apple gathering'), a hot spiced drink of cider and ale, with toast or pieces of apple floating in it. Each person takes out a piece and wishes good luck to everyone, before eating it and passing the cup on.

LAMMAS WOOL
4 large cooking apples
Honey
Nutmeg
4 pt. ale
Method
Core the apples and fill the centres with honey. Sprinkle with nutmeg and bake in the oven for 40 minutes in a deep baking tin. Remove from the oven and pour the ale over the apples. Heat gently on the hob for a few minutes, spooning the ale over the apples. Strain off the liquid and serve warm. The apples can be served separately.
AF

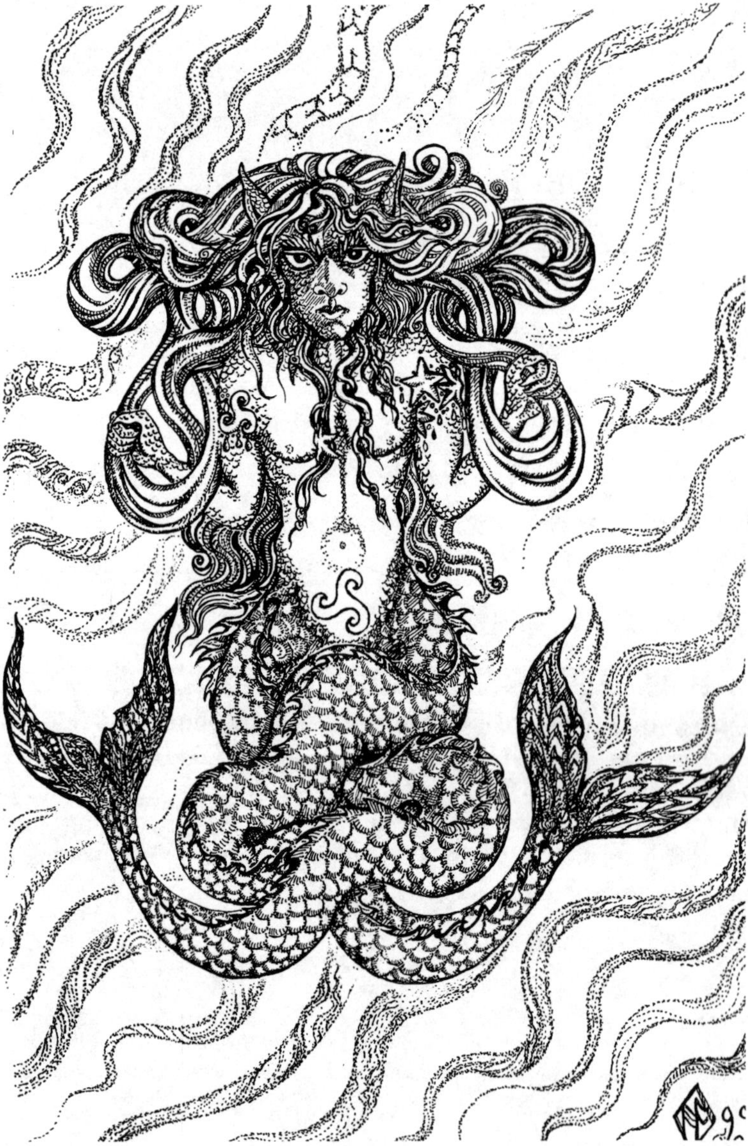

Chapter Six

Herfest

"*Memnosyne, Goddess of Memory, teach me what I once was, and what I yet may be.*"
Quote from the Eleusian Mysteries

TO MEMNOSYNE
Dreams flicker into life, light the unlived past,
Prompt the memories of a yesteryear when it seems I did not exist,
But which persist as phantom sympathies, eternally familiar.
Ghosts more real than transient time through which I now pass
My thoughts fly in many directions,
This life has formed in the bud, from a forgotten seed,
Buried in history, transferred, travelling.
I do not seek to be what I essentially am not.
I need to know my part in Nature's plan
That started when all things breathed as One.
Is personality alone- or is that illusion? Are we joined
In empathy with other souls, bringing realisation of all
That we have ever been, or will yet become?
PH

The Time of Completion

Herfest is celebrated at the Autumn Equinox and marks the completion of the harvest which began as early as mid June with the hay cutting. Light and darkness stand in balance, with equal hours of night and day; but the darkness is gaining, and with it, barren winter. We must look to the storing up of the provisions and the bounty of the earth. We give the Lord and Lady sincere thanks for what they have given to us, but also recognise that this is the time when the Lord leaves us as he dies with the cutting of the last sheaf of corn and begins his journey through the underworld. This is a time of great transformation.

Until recently the seasonal harvesters would elect a Harvest Lord empowered to negotiate with the farmer over terms and conditions on behalf of his fellows. As a symbol of his office, he would wear red poppies and bindweed around his hat. He would be served first at mealtimes and addressed as 'My Lord'. Originally in ancient times, he would have been the sacred king, elected for symbolic marriage with the land.

The corn harvest was fraught with tension. The weather might ruin the harvest, the work was hard and the final capture of the Corn Spirit was hazardous. The Corn Spirit had to be treated carefully to ensure a full rick. As late as the beginning of the twentieth century, the harvesters followed customs that would have been familiar to the ancient world. The corn was cut in decreasing circles, the Corn Spirit ever retreating into the remaining ears. There was a reluctance to be the one to cut the final ear and the be the captor of the spirit, so sickles were thrown at it from a safe distance. The final severance is called 'Crying The Neck' or 'Mare'.

Getting the harvest home safely was a time of great relief and a cause for celebration. A feast would be held for all the workers with an abundance of good food and drink and was probably the best meal the labourers would enjoy all year. The doors and gates of the farm were decorated with greenery, corn, flowers and ribbons and wreathed scythes and sickles would be placed in the arches of the house.

It must be remembered that Herfest is a dual festival, celebrating the harvest safely gathered in, but also the sacrifice and death of the Corn Lord who will sleep in the belly of Mother Earth until he rises again.

The expansive, active part of the year is over and it is time to turn inwards. Each festival of the year in its eternal spiral can be viewed as an initiation into a new mode of consciousness. At Herfest we enter into the death of the God. Through that death comes transformation, regeneration and rebirth. It is only through this process that spiritual illumination comes.

At Herfest we enter the Underworld part of the cycle of the wheel as the God enters the Underworld until his rebirth at Yule. It is the time for Otherworld travel and the exploration of the self. In the Underworld we encounter those aspects of the little self that stand in the way of the Initiation process. We are entering into the time of winter and darkness; the sun's powers waning. However, this it the time when, deprived of the external light, we encounter the inner illumination.
AF

Herfest Herb Craft
The apple symbolises the sun: as it ripens to yellow it is the passage of the sun across the sky; as it turns red it is the dying or setting sun which will rise anew each morning, reborn. For this reason the apple represents immortality. Legendary isles of apples are common, and always lie in the west, the place of the dying sun, from which it proceeds to enter the Underworld, or Land of Youth, travelling through the realms of death in preparation for its rebirth In the story

of King Arthur [originally a Celtic sun god], after he is mortally wounded, he is taken on a magic barge to the Isle of Avalon, which means 'Isle of Apples', from the Welsh afal meaning 'apple'. The Elysian Fields of the ancient Greeks, the place of the afterlife, also translates as 'apple orchards'. The western point of the circle marks the festival of Herfest, the setting of the sun at the autumn equinox, when the Lord dies and the dark days of winter begin.

The bean has been cultivated from ancient times in many parts of the world. The seed was thought to resemble the male testicle and the Egyptians made it an object of sacred worship and were forbidden to eat it. Jewish high priests were forbidden to eat beans on the day of atonement. In many cultures the flowers are associated with death and the spirits of the dead were thought to live in the blossoms. Beans were distributed and eaten during funerals; to this day in Italy beans dishes are eaten on the anniversary of the death of famous people. The bean represents the soul and its passage to the Otherworld after death, and it is traditional to eat beans at funeral feasts. At the autumn equinox, which marks the death of the God, a bean is baked into the harvest loaf and whoever finds the bean in their portion becomes Lord of the Feast and can command stories, songs and poems from the others, as well as being waited on with wine and food.

The hedgerows are bright with many fruits at this time of year, not the least the blackberry [*Rubus fructicosus*], a sacred plant of the Celts. In Scotland the bramble along with the rowan and the yew, constituted the sacred fire. In ogham the blackberry is an alternative for the vine, hence M - muin. A taboo on eating blackberries exists in Celtic countries, in Brittany and Cornwall the reason given is that the blackberry belongs to the fairy folk. The five petalled flowers associate the blackberry very strongly with the Goddess, and the fruit, which appears green at first, then red and finally black, represent the three stages of the Goddess and the completion of the cycle. Blackberries provide the wine at Herfest which marks the end of the harvest and completion. The Harvest Lord enters the Underworld at Herfest, the realm of the Sidhe, the fairy folk, the People of the Mounds, and is given into their care. The blackberry is a plant of the fairy folk, and the blackberries picked after the return of the dark time can be used to contact them. They can also be used for Underworld journeys, in the form of wines or cordials.

The hazel or cobnut [*Corylus avellana*] is Coll, one of the seven chieftain trees of Ogham. In Celtic legend nine hazel trees of poetry overhung the Connla's well. All the knowledge of the arts and science were given to these nine trees. The nuts, which had the property of giving wisdom, dropped into the well and were eaten by the salmon that swam there who developed one bright spot on his body for every nut he ate. These trees produced beauty (flowers) and wisdom (fruit) at the same time and eating the nuts from these trees conferred all knowledge and wisdom to the one that ate them. Nuts are a Celtic symbol of concentrated wisdom, the sweetness of knowledge contained, compact in a hard shell. Hence the expression 'the matter in a nutshell'. The hazel was associated with sacred springs and wells. The Celts saw water as one of the entrances to the Otherworld and offerings could be made to the gods by dropping hazelnuts into lakes and wells. Coll was the bardic number nine, as the hazel fruits after nine years. Nine is one of the most sacred numbers of the Goddess, three times three or the Triple aspect in triplicate. The hazel has connections with the festival of Herfest, the harvest festival celebrated in the ninth month of the year, when the tree produces nuts. It represents the fruition of what has gone before and the culmination of the work. Hazels should play a part in the Herfest festival and may be made into ritual cakes.

The elder [*Sambucus nigra*] is associated with witches and the Crone aspect of the Goddess, and it is often treated with

great caution and surrounded with warnings as a result. It is a tree of death; in megalithic burial chambers the funerary flints are the shape of elder leaves. Even the scent of elder was thought to bring death and disease. It was planted on new graves by the Welsh and Manx Celts; if it blossomed, the dead soul was thought to be happy in the land of Tir-nan-og. It is also a tree of regeneration because of its ability to re-grow damaged branches easily and to root and grow rapidly from any part.
AF

HARVEST LOAF
3 lb. wholemeal flour
1 tsp. salt
1 oz fresh yeast
1 $^1/_2$ pt. warm water

Method
Mix together the flour and salt and rub in the butter. Start off the yeast. Add to the flour mixture and stir in the water to make a dough. Knead well and return to the bowl. Cover with a clean cloth and leave in a warm place for 2 hours. Knead again, divide into 4 pieces and place in greased 1 lb. loaf tins. Cover again and prove for 30 minutes. Bake at 220ºC/425ºF/gas mark 7 for 30-40 minutes.

Traditionally the harvest loaf is plaited or shaped into wheat sheaf shapes and placed on trays for baking, rather than bread tins. We put a representation of John Barleycorn on top of the loaf and tear up the bread and throw pieces to each member of the group. Whoever gets John Barleycorn's 'special bit' becomes Lord or Lady of the feast and can order stories, entertainment, and food from the others.

BLACKBERRY WINE
4 lb. blackberries
1 lemon

2 lb. Sugar
Yeast
1 gallon boiling water
Method
Wash the fruit, place in a brewing bin and pour boiling water over it. Leave it for 3 days, stirring regularly. Strain the juice, dissolve the sugar in hot water and add to the mixture, together with the lemon juice. Cool to 20ºC and add the yeast. Transfer the must to a demi-jon and fit an airlock.

ELDERBERRY WINE
5 lb. elderberries
Juice and grated rind of 1 lemon
1 gallon water
Yeast
3 lb. sugar
Method
Strip the berries from the stalks with a fork. Put into a brewing bin and pour over 6 pt. of boiling water, mash down and stir in the lemon juice and peel. Cover and leave for 3 days, stirring daily, then strain into a demi-jon. Dissolve the sugar in 3 pt. of water and add this to the demi-jon. Cool to 20ºC and add the yeast. Fit an airlock and leave to ferment out. This wine needs to be kept at least 12 months before drinking.

HERFEST INCENSE
2 parts benzoin
2 parts myrrh
1 part hazel wood
$\frac{1}{2}$ part corn
$\frac{1}{2}$ part red poppy flowers
$\frac{1}{2}$ part cornflower
$\frac{1}{2}$ part ivy
Method
Blend together and burn on charcoal.
AF

Blessing of the Harvest Ritual

Take a loaf of bread and a goblet of wine and go out into the fields, orchard or garden. If this is not possible decorate the altar with the fruits of the harvest, corn, grapes etc.

Priest:
"Harvest begins; Earth once more yields
Her yearly ripeness from the golden fields.
The corn reflects the colour of the Sun, Lover
And Lord, who gave fertility to barren sward
And breathed the breath of joy
On winter's darkest heart,
And gave us all a part
In Love's Eternal Harvest.*

The priestess takes the bread.

Priestess: *"I do not only bless this bread, nor with it salt, Nor do I only bless the honey with the wine - I bless the body and blood and spirit of the Great Goddess, the Mother of the Corn, that she shall grant us a safe harvest and we shall know Her gentle spirit. In Her honour we hold this feast. Let us eat and drain the goblet deep and as we do, may we partake of Her blessings."*

Priest: [Holding the goblet of wine] *"I drink, yet it is not wine I drink, but the blood of the Goddess, since from wine it has changed into her blood and spread itself through the growing vines and trees, fruit ripening under the moon. I drink and salute the moon, praying that the Goddess will guard the grape until the harvest is complete. May it be good!"* [He drinks and passes the goblet on]

Priestess: [Holding the bread] *"I eat, but it is not bread I eat, but the body of the God, sprung from the womb of the earth, ripening under the sun. I eat and salute the sun, praying to the*

God that He will guard the corn until the harvest is complete, and His sacrifice made. May the crop be good!" [She eats and passes the bread on].

Wine and broken bread are scattered on the fields or into a dish of earth on the altar, later to be emptied onto the garden.

Priest: *"We have met this night to ask the Lord and Lady to bless the harvest, to give us plentiful crops to keep us through the dead time of winter. Let us remember their bounty and thank them for their gifts. Let this ritual end with love and blessings on us all. Blessed Be."*

All: *"Blessed Be"*
AF   * Invocation by PH

The Salmon

The salmon was regarded as a store of ancient knowledge and wisdom by the Celts and was one of the five oldest animals. The salmon is the king of the pool and can be very difficult to catch. It is also associated with deep wells and healing.

Conla's well [whose source was the river Boyne, named after the goddess Boann] was the source of poetic and literary style. In it lived several large salmon which fed on the hazelnuts which dropped into it. Each nut increased its wisdom and caused a red spot to appear on the salmon's back. In Celtic lore the hazel is the tree of wisdom, and the nuts represent knowledge in concentrated form. If a person were to catch and eat one of these salmon the wisdom would be transferred to them. Fish are still referred to as 'brain food'.

Fintan was the salmon of knowledge in Irish lore. Originally he was human and survived the great flood, hiding in a cave in salmon form for centuries, gaining wisdom and knowledge of all that went on in Ireland. The giant Finegas hunted it along the banks of the Boyne for seven years, eventually catching it and setting it to roast, watched by his pupil Fionn mac Cumhal. Fionn burned his finger on the hot flesh and placed in his mouth and thus acquired all the knowledge of the salmon. Afterwards he had only to place his thumb in his mouth to have foreknowledge of events.

In the story of the Irish hero Cuchulain he is bested in battle by his mistress Blathnat's husband, Curoi. Blathnat tricks the secret from Curoi that his soul is hidden in an apple in the belly of a salmon, and while it is there he cannot be killed. The salmon only appears once every seven years in a spring on the side of Slieve Mis. Furthermore, the apple can only be cut open by his own sword.

Cuchulain waits for seven years and catches the salmon and extracts the apple. Blathnat prepares a bath for her husband and then ties him up by his own hair, giving his sword to Cuchulain, who cuts the apple whereupon Curoi loses his strength and Cuchulain is able to cut off his head.

Particular salmon were considered to be the guardians of the wells or pools where they lived. If one of these were to be killed and removed from their well they would later revive, and make their way back to the pool, sometimes in human form. The salmon is said to live a very long time. One of Culhwch's tasks was to find the imprisoned god Mabon. He asked many birds and animals, each older and wiser than the last and in the end came to the salmon of Llyn Llyw, the most ancient of all, who told him where the god was.

In Norse myth Loki took the form of a salmon to flee from his fellow gods after the death of Baldur. The Gods used his own invention, a fishing net to catch him. Loki leapt high over the net but Thor caught him in his hands. He was bound to a rock to await the coming of Ragnarok, his writhings are said to cause earthquakes.

All traditions regard water as the element of life. The primordial waters are chaos but contain the potential of all life forms. Fishes are associated with fertility and creation. Fish was eaten at the feasts of the Mother Goddess on her day, Friday. It was a sacramental meal of the mystery religions associated with the ritual worship of moon goddesses of the waters and gods of the Underworld. As a fertility symbol the fish was also phallic. In Christian lore the early fathers were called pisciuli and fish were equated with the converted. Fish were given to feed the five thousand. Christ was depicted as a fish, ICHTHUS - Iesous CHristos THeou HUios Soter [Jesus Christ, son of god saviour]. Three intertwined fishes were borrowed from earlier religions to denote the Trinity. Bishops wore fish-head head-dresses: mitres. This lore was borrowed from the Sumero-Semitic Ea-Oannes, Lord of the Deeps, who was served by a priesthood in fish-head head-dresses. Fish was the eucharistic meal of Atargatis, her son Ichthys was the sacred fish.

The salmon was a popular form amongst Celtic shape changing magicians. Taliesin became a salmon in his battle with Cerridwen. In a similar story Tuan Mac Carill was eaten in salmon form by the wife of the king of Ireland and was once again reborn as a human. These are metaphors for initiation. The salmon can live in salt and fresh water and has perseverance and stamina in returning to its spawning grounds. Its pure willpower enables it to overcome many obstacles. However, salmon is very wise and instead of battling against the prevailing current uses a reverse current to swim upstream. The Irish hero Cuchulainn was said to be capable of the 'salmon leap' which enabled him to jump large obstacles and walls. Sometimes it is necessary to take an almighty leap into the unknown to gain knowledge.
AF

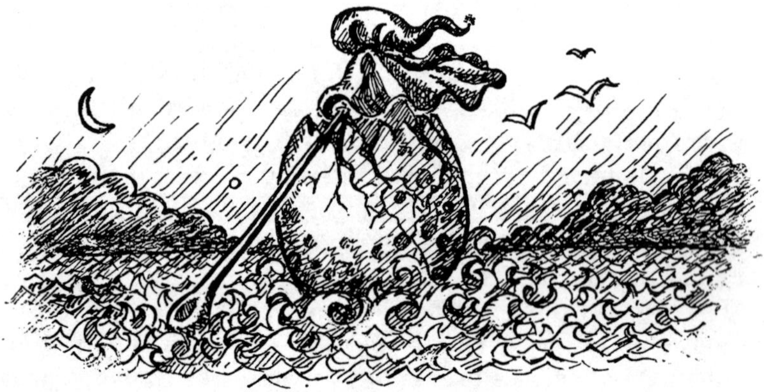

Salmon Pathworking
Relax.

You find yourself in an autumn landscape. The leaves are falling and the fields around you stand golden and ripe, ready for harvesting.

You are following the path of a clear, fast flowing river. As you walk along, you come to a still pool, surrounded by nine hazel trees. They drop their nuts into the pool.

As you watch, you see a large salmon come to the surface to feed on the nuts.

The autumn sun is warm and you long to slip into the pool and swim. You find yourself wading into the water and relaxing into its depths.

You swim easily, twisting and turning as easily as any fish. You can even breathe under water. Enjoy the unaccustomed freedom this gives you.

You see the light above you and move towards the surface of the pool.

Floating on it are the hazelnuts of concentrated wisdom. Eat one.

You become aware of the water as you move through it. You feel its ebb and flow. Though the current affects you, altering your course, but you don't care. You glory in its patterns and changes.

Be aware of the ebb and flow of life, sometimes calm, sometimes stormy. You see the patterns at work in your own life.

When you are finished, thank the salmon and return to the bank.

Let the scene fade around you and return yourself to waking consciousness.
AF

The Corn Dolly

It was believed that as the corn was harvested, the Corn Spirit retreated until it was embodied in the last remaining stems. The last stalks were ritually cut and woven into a corn dolly or kern maiden, sometimes called the Ivy Girl, which embodied the spirit of the corn. It was often tied with red thread for protective magic or symbolising blood and life, green thread symbolising fertility, brown for earth or yellow for the corn.

Sometimes the corn dolly was given a chair of honour at the harvest feast and would either be kept in the farmhouse until the next harvest or buried in the field with the crop sowing, thus returning the Corn Spirit to the earth and maintaining the cycle.

There are many patterns for making corn dollies, and these traditionally vary from region to region. A simple figure can be made as follows:

> 1. Take a sheaf of corn with ten to fifteen strands. Have ready some red thread.
>
> 2. Line up the bases of the seed heads and tie beneath them to make 'the hair' of the dolly.
>
> 3. About two inches below that, tie another thread to make the head.

4. Divide the rest into three pieces, with the greater amount in the central piece, which will form the body and the legs.

5. Tie off the ends of each arm and trim the corn level.

6. Tie some thread in the centre of the figure and divide the rest in half to make the legs.

7. Tie off each leg and trim level.
AF

The Cauldron

A cauldron is essentially a cooking pot, a vessel which transforms the raw ingredients of life into something new. There are many cauldrons in Celtic myth, owned by various gods and goddesses. Some mysteriously produce sustenance, some transform, some hold the fruits of the harvest or give life. In essence all these cauldrons represent the transformative womb of the Goddess, which may be the vault of the heavens or the underground earth, in which seeds germinate and growth, and return to in death to grow once more- the cycle of all life.

Perhaps the most famous story of a cauldron concerns the Goddess Cerridwen who brewed a potion which contained all the wisdom of the Three Realms. The cauldron simmered for a year and a day. A little boy, Gwion, was given the job of feeding the fire beneath it. One day three drops fell from the cauldron onto his finger, which he put into his mouth to ease the pain. Instantly he was at one with all things, past, present and future. Furious that he had stolen the magic, Cerridwen pursued him in the form of a black hag. Gwion, using his new powers, changed himself into a hare but Cerridwen turned into a greyhound to catch him. Gwion jumped into a river and became a fish while Cerridwen

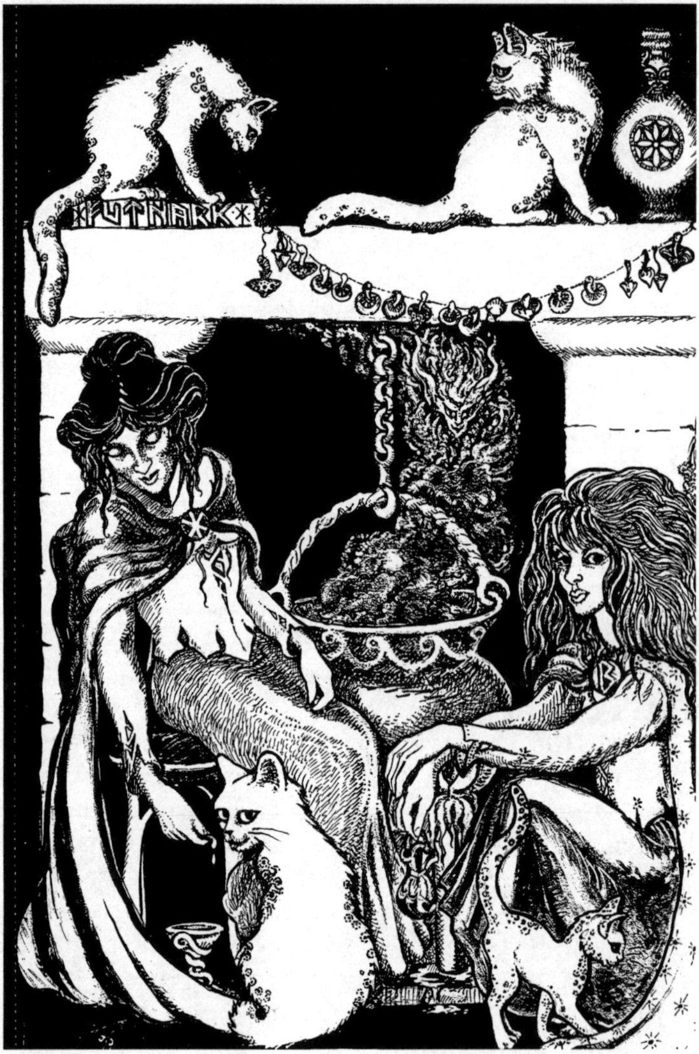
FUTHARK

proceeded to change herself into an otter and swam after him. He then flew from the river as a bird and Cerridwen became a hunting hawk. Hoping to elude her Gwion transformed himself into a grain of wheat on the threshing floor of a granary, but the goddess, becoming a black hen, ate him. For nine month Gwion remained in the womb of the goddess, until at last he was reborn as a beautiful boy child.

The story of Gwion relates the events of an initiation. First of all he stokes the cauldron of knowledge, then, when he least expects it, his consciousness is transformed. This all embracing knowledge then makes him afraid and he tries to run away from it. The goddess challenges him by assuming a frightening form to test his worthiness. He goes through different personifications of animal totems, assimilating the knowledge of different realities, while the confrontation of the goddess forces him on, refining his being. Eventually he has to be reassumed into the womb of the goddess in order to be reborn as a true initiate, one of the Twice Born.

Therefore the cauldron is a symbol of initiation, renewal, rebirth and plenty. It may contain water, fire, incense or flowers as the occasion demands. Leaping over the cauldron, like leaping over the broomstick, is a fertility rite.
AF

Consecrating a Cauldron
The cauldron is consecrated with an incense of chervil and primrose with the following worlds: 'God and Goddess, deign to bless this cauldron which I would consecrate and set aside. Let it stand for the cauldron which contained three drops of wisdom for all the world. God and Goddess, I call upon you to bless this instrument which I have prepared in your honour. Let blessing be' Use your new cauldron as soon as possible.
AF

Waves

In my dream the clouds look down on the castle. Silent, ruined, in many places without a roof, strength and vulnerability mingle in forlorn splendour. I watch as the sea wind stirs the grasses at my feet, out to the far horizon, blurred, indistinct. The wind blows my hair, what was once a gentle breeze hits my face with the smell of spray flung up from the rocks below. My mind shimmers through the still cloisters. Thoughts, dreams, memories. I sink into my emotions, and at once I am borne on the tide into a soft and secret sea. Gradually I swim away from the uncertainties of the past; mermaids pull me to rest and look in the oceanic womb of the Great Mother. To feel Her presence and peace.

I sense the inner tides of life, with which I have tried to blend. It has been like learning to swim, but more difficult. The mundane world has taunted me, scorned the wisdom of the past, ignorant of the subtle nuances of Dolphin's knowledge or the sagacity of the Salmon. My perception increases; like the ancestors I make the Salmon's leap. I know I am part of everything- Earth, Sky, and Sea, from whose waters all life has come.

The boiling cauldron of the longlost Beginning is before me; its steam rises upwards as the mist that hides our view of Avalon and the Cauldron of Annwyn. I sense the time of the single cell when perhaps the two worlds were One...

Then I swim into a reality where the pollution of modern times cannot reach, where the clear waters still nourish all beings. Where my disillusion is thrown up by the waves as a stone upon the sand. The warm sand greets me, swept clean.

On a rock, a distant figure calls to my thought. Manannan Lord of the Sea. The ocean still feeds and embraces us, as in my secret heart I feel the embrace of Manannan.
PH

AUTUMN HYMN

Summer's life is ebbing,
Leaves with russet glow
Still aflame with ardour
Wish their dreams to know.
Wind sighs through the branches,
Chills the sunlit scene;
Dappled gold discarded
Shows what might have been.

Mortal hopes of Summer
Lead to Winter's shade,
But the bright reflection
That will never fade
Lingers in the moonlight,
Mirror of the sun,
Till that warmth embrace us
When our race is won.

PH

Persephone

In classical myth Persephone was captured and taken by Hades, the God of the Underworld to his realms. Her mother, the corn goddess Demeter sought her all over the length and breadth of the land, mourning all the time for the loss of her daughter, and refusing to make the earth blossom and bear fruit. The land became barren and wasted and the people cried out to the gods for succour. At last, weary she sat down for nine days and nights, and the gods caused poppies to spring all around her feet. Breathing in the soporific perfume she feel asleep and rested.

The Gods bargained with Hades that Persephone should be returned to her mother, as long as she had eaten no food in the Underworld. However, she had eaten three seeds of a pomegranate, and was therefore doomed to spend three months each year in the underworld, during which time winter fell upon the earth.

Poppies, which grow along with corn, are an emblem of Demeter, Goddess of the harvest, and Persephone, the seed corn in the earth, which grows in the spring and returns to the Underworld at the harvest.
AF

RANDOM HARVEST

I look for you throughout this weary world,
Who once knew you in fair Elysium;
Persephone, a lost child of our times,
Waif of the dawntide of millennium,
Knowing that, Demeter, your tears bathe
Trembling Earth that waits your harvest swathe.

Once long ago our hearts were young and glad;
All worlds, all Nature, seemed in harmony.
But now a pall of ignorance and fear
Casts a sad shadow on Earth's destiny.
Once more be a mother to the lost.
Sunlight strengthens broken lives, storm-tossed.

A mother's love enfolding two as One-
Our planet held within dimensions fair;
An image, clearer than all argument
Of Man, in Cosmic tides, yet unaware.
Hellenic wisdom still holds wide the door
To deathless vistas, Heaven's golden store,
Beyond the narrow rainbow of our sense,
Yet still within Love's touch and cognisance.
PH

SAGA OF THE SUNSET

Who sails with me?- far from this Northwind land
Of ice and fire, whose steaming cauldrons boil
From hidden hell- the place of dark and light
Whose lissom demons leap into the night
To join the sun-swept sky in whirling phantasy.

Who sails with me? Away from sheltering shore;
Those lands explored hold no more stark surprise.
But through the mists, across the poisoned sea
There is another place - the sagas say,
Of fruited vines and gold and silver panoply.

Where dragons sport across an endless plain,
And tall trees grow whose branches touch the sky;
I sense this voyage is our destiny-
We leave our Motherlands where pillared ice
Stands crystalled sentinel of our domain.
The serpent ships, whose wombs bear us all
Beyond the frontier of our ancient night-bound sand,
Dream silent, of their crunching hulls on alien strand.

Within this western vale the seasons meet;
Summer and Winter in perpetuity.
The cold familiar- and a torrid heat-
The Sun reigns here, Incarnate, so I've heard tell.
But I, a Viking, born of heaven and Hell,
Am proved your leader, as you all know well.
If not this shore, then to Valhalla let it be-
Once more I ask, then I command - Who sails with me?

We dare not seek to plunder this unknown
So long elusive to mere human ken,
Whose women are the daughters of the stars-
Whose yielding to us still may prove us men.
If by the power of Odin we set sail,
Then in His wisdom let them be unfurled.

Around our dragon-prows the tides will stream
That have borne within another world.
Across our bows the sunset tints the spray
A dancing mist-veil of lightfeathered day.
The strength of Gods is in my blood, a crimson sea-
I, Odin's son, repeat my cry: 'Who sails with me?'
PH

Chapter Seven

Samhain

SAMHAIN HYMN
Deep the night and cold-
The earth, caught
In Winter's hard embrace
Escapes, teasing,
Remembering Summer-
Autumn leaves dance, shivering.

The energy that drives the stars
Disseminates.
All Nature waits,
Anticipates
Vernal rebirth
From the dark womb of the Earth.

And we, my love, children of the Gods,
Whose bond, nurtured in secret,
Was tossed by life's storms,
Now hide in Winter's mantle,
Wrapped in ghostly mist,
Which brings forth
The green buds of endless Spring.
PH

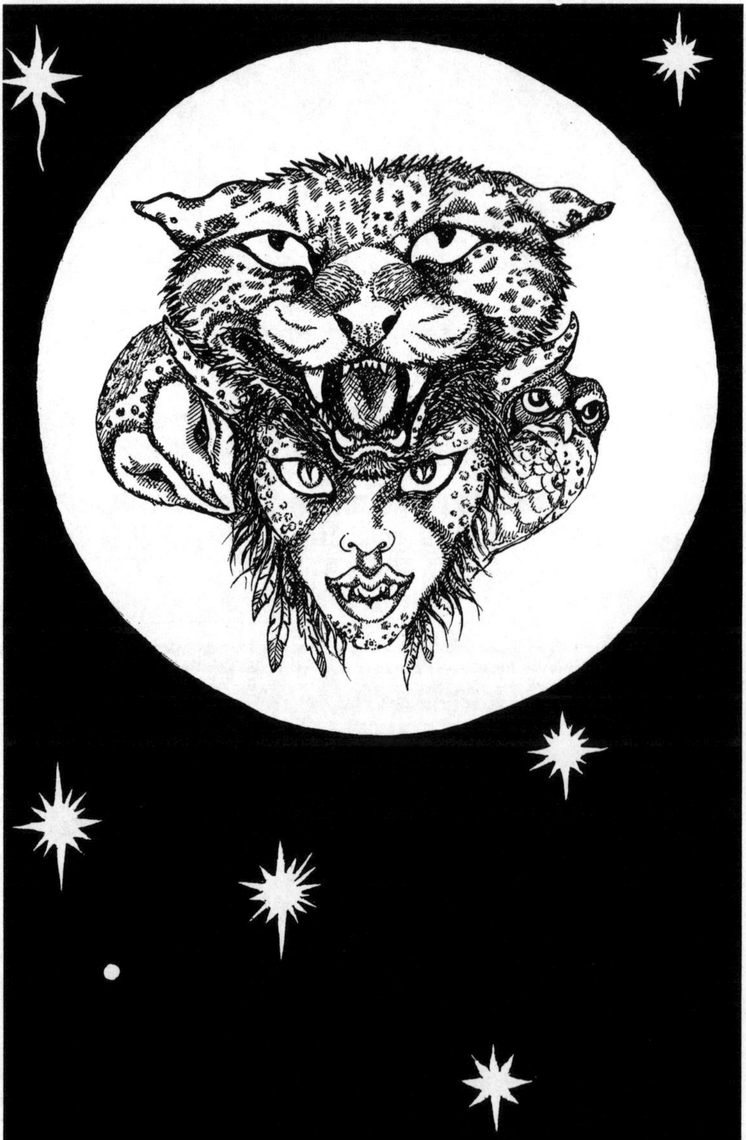

Samhain

Every year, on October 31st we celebrate Halloween or All Hallow's Eve, when the ghosties and ghoulies are supposed to come out from under the bed and the cracks in the woodwork. We hollow out pumpkins and turnips and put lighted candles in them and place them in the windows. There is a delicious frisson of light hearted fear in the air and the festival features in many horror stories.

The festival is very ancient and stems from the Celtic festival of Samhain. The Celts recognised only two seasons- the start of summer, which was celebrated at Beltane [May Day] and winter, which started at Samhain, the 1st November. The hours of light have diminished; the days are short. The harvest has been gathered in, leaves fall from the trees and animals ready themselves for hibernation. The powers of growth and light are in decline, seemingly ready to fall into their long winter sleep of death. The powers of darkness and cold begin to gain ascendancy.

It may seem a strange time to begin the marking of a new year, this time of death and darkness before the coming of new life, growth and light; for the ancients, however, existence was a wheel, a cycle of birth, growth, death and rebirth. Before birth must come death, not an evil horror, but a just and natural part of the cycle. For the Celts, in all calculations of time, night preceded day, thus Samhain night [oidhche Samhain] was the night preceding Samhain, not the night after. We still encompass this idea in our word 'fortnight'. So the dark days of winter precede the light of summer.

For the Celts any boundary was important magically, it could be a place between places, like the strand between shore and sea, or a time between times, like dawn and dusk. In folk memory the watch between midnight and one is still called 'the witching hour', because this too is a transition between one day and another. These times and places were dangerous, one might enter the Otherworld through them accidentally, or the Otherworld might pass through into out own. The time when one season passed to another was particularly tricky, especially the two hinges of the year, Beltane and Samhain, when the Otherworld came very close. Samhain is the pivotal point of the year itself, when one year passes to the next, and the doors between the worlds stand open.

The Celts believed that because the veils between the worlds are thin at this time, the spirits of the ancestors were close. Hence the idea of ghosts issuing forth at Halloween. Indeed, the whole period between Samhain and the rebirth of the sun at the winter solstice [around 21st December] was a tricky time when spirits were abroad, it was their period of the year. So Christmas too was a popular time for ghost stories and legends- think of the Christmas stories of Dickens and M.R. James, with their strong supernatural element. This custom has largely died out, but until just a few years ago the BBC screened a ghost story every Christmas Eve.

Samhain began the Celtic new year, and the Celtic inhabitants of the Isle of Man still celebrate Hogmanay at this time. All household fires were put out on Samhain Eve, and the population would gather on a nearby hilltop where a large bonfire would have been prepared the previous day. There they would wait in silence and darkness until the hour was past between the seasons and the spirits which roamed abroad had departed. Then the sacred needfire would be lit. The time of danger past, everyone would celebrate and make merry. When the dawn came, each family would then take a torch from the sacred fire to rekindle their own fire from, thus marking an ending and a beginning: the end of summer, and the beginning of winter. The fires themselves were a means of purification, of expelling evils. Cattle were driven through the ashes to free them from disease. The fire was sympathetic magic to encourage the weakening sun. This is the true origin of the Bonfire Night fires, rather than the Gunpowder Plot, which was grafted onto the custom. Samhain fires were lit until quite recent times in the Highlands and in Wales, where people would jump through the fire, and when it had burnt down, rush away to escape the 'black sow', the death goddess, who would take the hindmost.

At Samhain the cattle were brought down from the summer pastures to the safer winter ones. Any beast that could not be kept through the winter would be slaughtered. This is one of the reasons Samhain was called 'the festival of the dead'. It may have been that some of the animals would have been ritually sacrificed to propitiate the powers of winter [like Irish offerings at Samhain to the Formorians, Gods of Blight], and to feed the spirits of the dead that came to visit the Samhain feast. To this day a traditional Scottish food at this time is blackbread and oatcakes mixed with blood instead of water. Possibly one of the animals would have been made 'scapegoat', carrying all the evils of the previous year.

Many 'Halloween' customs of secular society are a race memory - the sacred pumpkin or hollowed out root of the druids, carved with a frightening face and lit from within to keep the spirits away, the burning of the clavie in Scotland, balefires on the Carn nam Marbh [mound of the Dead] and the bonfires of early November, which pre-date the supposed festival of Guy Fawkes by thousands of years.

Winter in ancient times was hard. Animals for whom there was not enough fodder would have to be slaughtered. Many people would die; the old, the sick, the very young. If the harvest had been poor even the strong would not survive. Death was always close. At this time too plant life withers and dies, the earth will shortly become bare. However, ivy, holly and other evergreens carried the spirit of life throughout the winter, and promised the renewal and rebirth of the spring.

For the ancients the earth was the body of the Mother Goddess and any hollows in the earth, such as caves and wells, represented her womb. Life grew from the womb of the Mother, the land itself, and in death was laid back into the earth as a tomb, which in turn became the womb of rebirth. The harvest is collected, the seed laid into the earth and in the spring new life grows. Neolithic man built burial mounds to house his dead. Bodies were placed in the tombs in the foetal position, awaiting rebirth from the womb of the Goddess. These chambers were sometimes built in the shape of the Goddess herself. At Samhain the spirits were said to issue forth from the hollow hills; the ancestors return to speak with the living.
AF

GEIMREDH (WINTER)
Drifting like cobwebs in the tide of time,
Memories, promise if Summer-
As the cold grips all Nature
Our beings shiver, seek out warmth.
But we found what ever burns within the stars,
Too deep for earthly encompassing,
Whose wild elements bring the fruits
Of Eternal Spring.

Grieving for lost hopes, broken human dreams,
Forgetting the sun in winter-
Light as a snowflake touching;
Still it will live unconquered.
Time cannot destroy the inner fire
Sifting through all the remembering;
In it a promise still lives,
As the yet unborn.

> Gods of my youth, my age and my life,
> Your touch enfolds me forever;
> Sure the primeval pattern
> Of all that was and will be.
> I sense within the Samhain mists
> The Summer flower in me blossoming -
> Still upon the Winter rose
> Gleams the dew of dawn.
> PH

Hunter's Moon Meditation

Relax.

You find yourself on a hillside in the light of an October moo,. The season is drawing towards winter and you see this reflected in the landscape around you.

Ahead of you you can make out a longbarrow, shaded by an elder tree. A few remnants of berries and leaves cling to it, and around the trunk ivy twines. You are drawn by the burial mound and walk towards it.

As you near it, you see something glinting on the ground at the doorway. As you bend to pick it up, you see that it is a golden apple, a passport to the underworld, the realms of the sidhe.

From inside the barrow you hear the sound of voices and laughter. These become still as a rumbling sound from deep within the earth grows, coming nearer and nearer towards you; the pounding of horses' hooves and the baying of hounds. A hunting horn winds its eerie cry as crashing from the barrow the Wild Hunt emerges. Led by Herne the Hunter, dark wrapped and horned, horses and dogs rush into the night, and away into the hills. They see your golden apple and ride past you, not interfering with you.

Startled you stand back, but as you do, curious beautiful faces peer out of the burial chamber at you. They are the sidhe, the people of the mounds. You hold up the apple and they welcome you into the barrow.

As you enter, you realise the tunnels curve and descend, deep into the earth: a labyrinth. However, the Fair Folk lead you to a chamber, aglow with golden light, where dozens of them are feasting. A cup, made of ivy wood is passed to you and you quaff a heady brew, wondering at the smiles of the one who gives it to you.

It is a cup that gives visions. You have entered the underworld where the God rests until the time of his rebirth, only riding out on windy nights with the Wild Hunt. The folk of the mounds have welcomed you in and given you the cup of wisdom, brewed in the cauldron of Cerridwen.

Explore now the visions of the Goddess Cerridwen, of life and death and rebirth.

[Pause for about ten minutes.]

The visions fade around you, and you are surprised to find yourself back on the hillside, outside the mound. The sun is rising in the mists on the horizon. Within the barrow all is still, apart from the faint echoes of laughter.

When you are ready, thank the sidhe and bring yourself back to waking consciousness.
AF

Candles

Candles have been used by mankind for thousands of years. The word is derived from the Latin *candere* which means 'to flicker' or 'to glow' and until the Victorian Age candles and lamps provided the only form of lighting known to mankind. Candles have been made from many things. For the less well heeled, cheap candles were made from tallow, or rendered animal fat. Though effective, these candles tended to smoke and were somewhat smelly. The best candles have always been made from beeswax, and this is still the most popular material in use today. No candle can work without a wick and again, various materials have been used. In the past both reeds and flax have been used, though plaited cotton is more commonly used today.

Candles, representing the light of the spirit, are an important part of many rituals. Three candles are usually placed on the altar - we use white, red and black to represent the three phases of the moon and the Triple Goddess, and candles are placed in the four quarters of the circle [north, east, south and west]. In addition different colours are used for different purposes:

Black: Samhain, ancestor contact, the Crone Goddess, the void or womb, receptivity, Scorpio, Capricorn

Blue: Herfest, the west, water, healing, spiritual protection, tranquillity, throat chakra, third eye chakra, Moon, Virgo, Aquarius

Brown: Herfest, earthiness, practicality

Gold: Coamhain, spiritual energy, strength, life force, solar plexus chakra, Sun

Green: Beltane, Yule, the North, earth magic, fertility, prosperity, love, compassion, heart chakra, Venus, Cancer, Capricorn

Grey: communication, Mercury

Indigo: intuition, vision, insight, third eye chakra, Taurus

Orange: Samhain, Lughnasa, success, Sun, courage, self esteem, spleen chakra, Leo,

Magenta: inspiration, creative vitality, base chakra

Pink: Handfastings, love, beauty, harmony, peace, heart chakra, Libra

Purple: Occult power, Pisces

Red: Yule, Coamhain, the south, fire, energy, vitality, sexual energy, base chakra, the Mother Goddess, Mars, Aries

Silver: Esbats, communication, personal enlightenment, Moon

Turquoise: creativity, communication, throat chakra

Violet: spirituality, self esteem, spiritual growth, third eye chakra, crown chakra, Sagittarius

White: Imbolc, dispelling negativity, the Maiden Goddess, purity, cleansing, protection, crown chakra

Yellow: Ostara, the East, development of the mind and intellectual capacities, vision, solar plexus chakra, Mercury, Leo

Making Candles

The best candles are made from pure beeswax, though paraffin wax is more common. Stearin is added to the wax at a rate of about 10% to harden it. The wax mixture must be heated in a double boiler or in one saucepan heated over another of simmering water. Commercially available dyes or children's wax crayons can be added to the melted wax to colour your candles.

The diameter of the wick needs to be adjusted to take into account the size of the candle, If the wick is too narrow, the candle will puddle and go out. If the wick is too wide, the candle will smoke.

The type of perfume that you can buy to scent candles is all synthetic, and is of no magical value. If you want to perfume magical candles you will need to add pure essential oil, which can be done just before the wax is poured.

There are many ways of shaping candles and you can be as creative as you like. Here are a couple of simple methods:

1] One of the easiest ways of making a candle is in a mould. There are many varieties commercially available, constructed from metal, glass, flexible PVC, rubber and plastic, though you can use household items such as yoghurt pots, tin cans and so on.

Thread a wick through a small hole in the bottom of the mould and knot it. At the top of the mould suspend a twig and tie the other end of the wick to it. Pour in the melted wax and after a minute tap the sides of the mould to release any air bubbles. Stand the whole thing in a bath of cold water, placing a weight on top to keep it down. Check it after an hour and top up with more wax if necessary. When the candle has set remove it from the bath and cut off the know at the bottom and pull the candle out of the mould. Cut off the wick to the required length. If the bottom of the candle is uneven, 'iron' it off in a hot saucepan.

The candle can then be painted, or you can make patterns in the surface with the back of a hot spoon or with a warm knife. You can also decorate the candle with dried, pressed flowers: take your flowers and lay them on the candle then 'iron' all over with the back of a hot spoon.
AF

Consecrating Candles

Candles are anointed with an essential or infused oil from a plant suitable to the purpose from the centre to the top and then the centre to the bottom with the words:

> '*Be to me the fire of moon,*
> *Be to me the fire of night,*
> *Be to me the fire of joy,*
> *Turning darkness into light.*
> *By the virgin waxing cold,*
> *By the Mother full and bold,*
> *By the Hag Queen, silent, old,*
> *By the Moon, the One in Three,*
> *Consecrated, Blessed Be.*'

November Ritual

The hours of darkness are now short indeed and night comes early. Some call this the Dead Month, because the sun is dying and so is the plant life around us and we have yet to look forward to the lengthening of daylight after the winter solstice, bringing with it the promise that spring will eventually return. It is time to call upon those things which see us through the dark times, the produce stored for the winter, the light of the candles and the warmth of the fire,

little brothers of the sun.
The sacred space is made.

Priest: *"Now is the time of the winter dark. We call on the Lord and lady to keep us safe through this time. Let the candles be lit in token of this."*

Priestess: [Lighting the altar candles and then blessing all the altar candles which will be used for the coming year.]

> *"Be to me the fire of moon,*
> *Be to me the fire of night,*
> *Be to me the fire of joy,*
> *Turning darkness into light,*
> *By the virgin waxing cold,*
> *By the mother, full and bold,*
> *By the hag queen, silent, old,*
> *By the moon, the one in three,*
> *Consecrated, Blessed Be."*

Purification Ritual

The leaves are falling from the trees and winter is fast approaching. It is time to prepare practically and spiritually for the dark time of the year. Most people have probably spent the last few weeks making sure their house is ready for the winter cold, painting, repairing, storing wood [or electric cards!] and preserving produce.

Spiritually it is also time to prepare for the difficult time ahead. The following is a ritual of personal purification which should be performed when the moon wanes after the Winter Moon of October. Samhain is the Pagan new year and it is time to let go of the old and during this underworld part of the cycle [up until Yule] to undertake deep inner journeys.

Prepare your special place of working by cleaning it thoroughly and set up your altar and candles at each of the quarters. On the altar place a fireproof dish and a lit white candle, several pieces of paper and a pen.

"I call upon the Old Ones, the ancient Gods, to witness this ritual and hear my intent. The year is dying and I come to watch it pass. With its passing I release these things:"

Sit down before your altar and bring to mind those things you have done in the past year of which you are ashamed or regret, perhaps things that have hurt other people or indeed, yourself. When you are ready take the first piece of paper and make a symbol on it that represents one thing. Summon it to mind and project it into the symbol, then burn it in the candle flame and let it go, when it is burnt it is done with. Take the next piece of paper and do the same with the next regret and so on. Take as long as you like and use as many pieces of paper or symbols as you like.

"Witch Lady, Witch Lord, you have witnessed my actions and seen into my heart, I call upon you to guide me in the future, help me to live by your law and harm none. Your true worship lies within the heart that rejoiceth, all acts of love and pleasure are your rituals. Let there be beauty and strength, power and compassion, humour and humility, mirth and reverence within me. I thank you for your presence and ask you to be with me all my days, lighting my path. Let this ritual end in love and blessings. The rite is ended, blessed be."
AF

Imprisonment

Imprisonment - does any other word evoke more thoroughly the loneliness of the human soul? We may be surrounded by light and laughter, but conscious that no other present can imagine the emptiness that longs to blend, the recognition of dreams shared and understood. But if anyone can know another's being, bridge their solitude, instil realisation into their mind, the prison dissolves and wholeness is possible. Perhaps only one can share, perhaps many more. The prison of oneself is not without worth- it enshrines what is sacred to that person, showing only to those who are capable of insight.

There are so many kinds of prison- where people are hostage to their own mistakes [deliberate or otherwise], or illness, grief, or regret. Burdened by sorrow for what might have been, encumbered by guilt, we struggle on, wondering if there is a gateway out of life's prison, wondering where it would lead if we found it. Into the many paths of bewildering advice, hope, or illusion. Where are the certainties? As we grow older the world itself can be a jail; one can long to reach out to an immortal hope through the bars of fear, ignorance, delusion and experience.

As weakness replaces strength we crave for energies to empower our frail bodies. But everything has its price. Spend too much of your substance, wallow too freely in the virtual reality called existence and its prison begins to firm its doors. But are you quite incarcerated? The rivers blend with the ocean, the clouds with the air. Sunlight shines in the dense forest, giving it renewal. Love may be the link that binds the universe, or perhaps we need another word for it. But this link is not a chain that binds, it bends. Some call it God or Goddess, personified at times in Nature, in thought, in dreams, and represented in us. Some think there is a Divine presence, some not, but the latter have the worst penal servitude, since within all dilemmas we find creeds professing Divine guidance. Comfort must be larger than existence. Existence itself gives us no quarter. We are victims, but we might be survivors. If there is a key to turn, and the prison door is unlocked, one day we may walk away free.
PH

The Wall

Many years ago I read a science fiction story, the plot of which concerned a man who wished to know what was on the other side of a mysterious wall. There were many legends about it; people regarded it with dread. It encircled his planet and one day, he and his friend decided to climb it. As he traversed it, his unease gradually became less, until the final discovery- it possessed only one side. That might have been all, except for the impossible convoluted path...

This was naturally food for thought. The idea does not apply to any natural law on earth - or any supernatural one. Nevertheless, the reference to the 'twisted loop' in many ancient religions seemed some sort of key. The possibility that reality can twist or loop makes sense to me. The world that the Celts knew as Tir Nan Og and the Greeks as Elysium might be as real as our own. A path that leads from here to there, twisting like a coil of string, like the twine with which Ariadne lead Theseus out of the labyrinth. Or a piece of paper folded so that two sides become one.

Why does Nature hide her secrets so that what we see is anything but the whole picture? Unlike our ancestors, we know the answers to such questions as where do stars go in the daytime? Where is the round moon when it is new?

Belief in the fairy world, once called 'the secret commonwealth' was, and is, widespread. In Britain, as in all Celtic countries, that world seemed particularly close; at dawn and dusk, at the climactic point of the seasons, especially at Samhain or Halloween. In this century beliefs have been eroded by scientific thinking, uncertain steps of faith pushed backwards, now science itself is trembling on its path to enlightenment, making its first tracks on the road to Elysium. Will it get there alone? I think not. Visionaries from all over the world - and beyond- may lend a helping hand.

Many of us make a personal journey, to learn more of ourselves, to find a meaning to life. I have made that journey, so far an uncertain one, but one where clues were many, the evidence strong. I am not a person to whom faith in anything comes naturally, something I share with many of my contemporaries; children of the troubled years before the Second World War and its disillusioned aftermath. Our worldview was shattered by humankind's tragedy, which saw the whole of Nature as being surrounded by a wall, beyond which we can sense nothing. Only recently has science recovered its sense of awe and its own ignorance. Where there is a will to learn, there is hope.

All our ancestors had a sense of wonder. They asked how and why. Their traditions still live. The enigmas we face are the same. The answers may be blowing in the solar wind...

CLASS OF '47
It seems all dreams are at an end;
They end, like life, in Winter.
What did our trembling hopes portend?
Must this world split and splinter?
Naive and young, ideals not lost,
We started our ascent
Of time's unyielding pyramid;
O'er rough-hewn stone we went.

The earth is sad, its people still
Beset with fears and sorrows.
Was it presumptuous of us,
The wish to build tomorrows
Where no-one in the world would grieve
Without some intuition
Of Life Eternal, where Earth's seed
Would blossom in fruition?

> Now radio, TV, streak the skies,
> Pour messages to Heaven,
> And somehow in a million sighs
> An echo of lost truth replies:
> The dawn-star leads a new sunrise,
> Which did our questing minds surprise
> And youth and promise dared surmise
> In nineteen-forty-seven.
> PH

Rite For Samhain

Samhain marks the pivotal point of the year, when summer turns to winter. It is the most powerful 'time between times' of all, when the veils between the worlds are thin, and the spirits of the Ancestors are sought for their guidance.

The candles are orange and black and the altar is decorated with rowan berries, apples and lighted pumpkins. The beacon or tapers are traditionally made from mullein stems. The fire is lit from elder, apple, blackthorn and juniper wood. Apples and cider may be substituted for the cakes and wine.

The High Priestess casts the circle, lights the beacon at the North-West point of the circle and leads the chant:

> *Power of stone and power of earth,*
> *Power that shapes our place of birth,*
> *Spin the wheel of night and day,*
> *Spin the wheel OR-AH-AY.*

> *Power of ice and water free,*
> *Power that hides the depths of sea,*
> *Weave the web of night and day,*
> *Spin the wheel OR-AH-AY.*

Power of wind and power of air,
Power of mountains bleak and bare
Turn the time of night and day,
Spin the wheel OR-AH-AY.

Power of flame and power of fire,
Power of all our vast desire,
Light of dark and light of day,
Spin the wheel OR-AH-AY.

The High Priestess then calls on the Ancestors:

"Harken to the voice of our souls and hear us. Harken for we call upon those who have passed from this life, back through the generations of man to the time of our first parents. We light the beacon that you are guided to this place and we call upon you. Listen to the voice of our souls, all those of the past. Harken to us, those who shall be of our house. The gulf between the worlds is narrow at this time. Approach all those who were of this house. Come, those who are of this house. Come, those who will be of this house. Come and share our joy this night. Let the cup be filled in the name of the Three, for we would speak once more to those who have passed from us and we would see those who are yet to be. Come to us and rejoice."

There is a silence in order to allow the Ancestors to communicate with those present.

The High Priestess then makes the invocation to the Goddess:
"Queen of the midnight skies, we rejoice in thy blessing. We call on thy maiden beauty to bless us with insight and serenity. We invoke thy silver graciousness to light the ways of lovers and guard the sleep of children. We call upon thy dark aspect this night, the Lady of the Dead and the Unborn show us in this darkness thine understanding and grant us, Lady, blessing. Descend unto the body of thy servant and priestess. Come, Lady, come........"

She takes the cup of wine :

"Dark Queen, bless the wine in this cup in token of the cauldron which contained three drops of wisdom for all the world. Creatures of earth and creatures of water, creatures of air and creatures of fire, friends in life and friends in death, gather here in the Dark Queen's name."

The wine and the wisdom of the cauldron is shared. Divination of various kinds may then be employed to seek guidance for the coming year. New members and initiates are brought forward and presented to the First Parents as newborns in the House. The plans for the coming year are discussed. There is feasting within the circle in the presence of the ancestors and the Gods which continues until dawn is breaking. When all is completed the High Priestess gives the Farewell Before Dawn:

"We have rejoiced this night in the knowledge that time is no barrier and that friendship endures. Yet the hours of the feast draw to their close and time brings this feast to its end. Therefore go to your appointed places disturbing not those who would fear you, nor harming any substance of this world. Remember that we will meet again some other Hallow's Eve, so let it end with love and blessings on us all."

The circle is closed.

AF

Chapter Eight

Yule

YULETIDE HYMN
Midpoint of the darkness
Sheltering the Infant Sun
Whose eyes look for the gentle candle glow
That His own essence shares.

He will grow strong,
And give once more to our shivering bodies,
Our lost yearnings, our broken hearts
The renewal Earth borrows
From the Wheel of Time,
In which the stars turn.
In which we reflect something
Of all the seasons, all the lives,
All the hopes, all the uncertainties,
All the dreams, that have ever been.
PH

The Midwinter Solstice

This is the festival of Yule or wheel, falling on the midwinter solstice, the darkest day of the year. It has been celebrated since the dawn of time, from the Roman Saturnalia and the Saxon fire festivals to the Christian festival of Christmas, the birth of Jesus Christ.

Solstice means the sun 'stands still', and the winter solstice in our northern hemisphere occurs when we are tilted at the

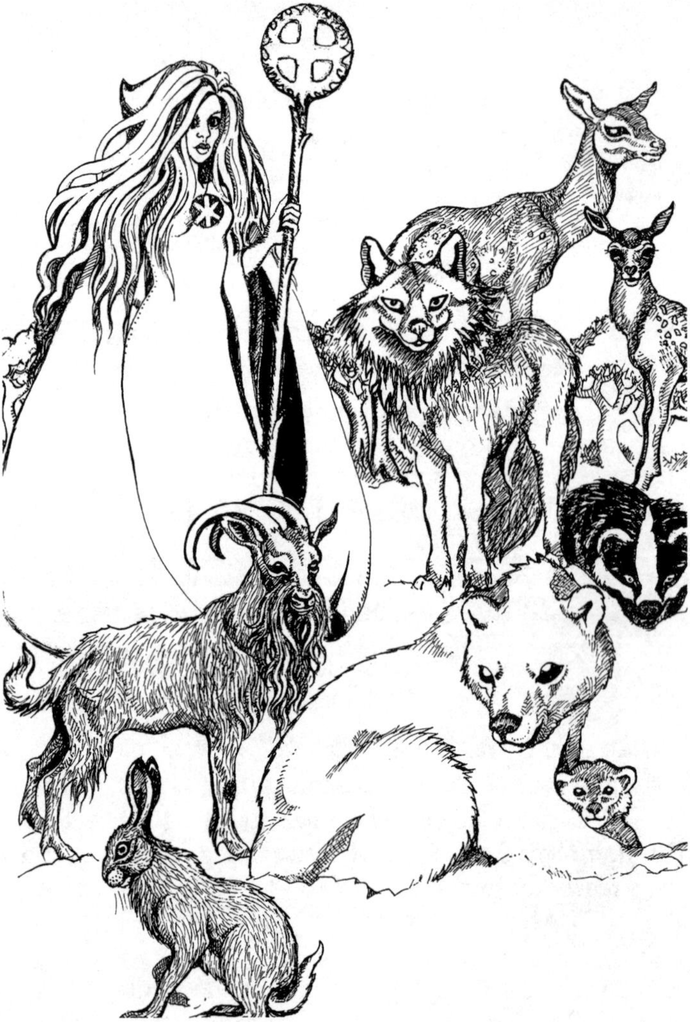

furthest point from the sun. The midwinter solstice is the shortest day, with only about six hours of daylight remaining, and the longest night of the year, After the solstice the sun grows stronger and the days lengthen, until its zenith at the midsummer solstice, the longest day and shortest night.

To many the sun was, or represented a god, and the diminishing of his warmth and light over the winter months was seen as his sickness and decline towards death. It was important to banish the darkness before the sun disappeared forever. For the ancients, the rebirth of the sun was by no means certain. Humans believed that they partook in the cycle of the wheel, their actions affecting it. Their efforts and rituals were needed to turn it, and ensure the regeneration of the god. Unless prayers were said, ceremonies performed, sacrifices made there would be no return of the sun, no summer, no harvest.

Winter was a dangerous time, not only from the threat of death by cold or starvation, but because between the dark days of Samhain and Yule the dead walked the land. It was a time for ghosts, werewolves, vampires and the wild hunt. Charms and spells were needed to protect people, animals and property, fire was need to push back the darkness. In Greece a black bull, wreathed in yew was sacrificed to Hecate to appease the dark spirits. Yew is an evergreen still associated with the solstice, it is known as a tree connected with the spirits and with death [churchyards are planted from yew, bows were made from yew, arrows were poisoned with a poisonous decoction from the needles and berries].

Fire is the brother of the sun, so fires were lit at the solstice to encourage [by sympathetic magic] the sun to strengthen and begin the long climb back to midsummer. Around the fire would dance shaman dressed in deer skins and antlers, goat hide and horse head skulls and masks. Red was worn to give strength to the sun.

The sun was reborn from the Underworld or the womb of the Goddess. The Sheila na gig represents the Earth Mother giving birth to the midwinter sun. Many chambers such as the one at Newgrange are oriented to the midwinter solstice. The sun illuminates the inner chambers and appears to re emerge from it as though emerging from the cave womb of the Goddess. According to legend the sun god Lugh is buried at Newgrange i.e. it is his tomb and womb of rebirth. Spirals carved around the entrance depict the path of the sun, spiralling down to death and out again from kits rebirth, thus the spiral becomes the symbol for rebirth.

In the northern hemisphere traditions many gods of the sun and light are said to have been from a cave, for example Mithras, the Persian god of light was born in a cave on December 25th. Zeus the chief god of the Greeks was born in a cave on the darkest night. The Cretans maintained he was born every year in the same place with flashing fire and a stream of blood. This indicates that he was originally a sun god.

The Celts regarded the sun that rose on the day before the solstice as a shadow sun, the real sun being by Arawn the king of the underworld. In a year of thirteen lunar months of twenty eight days there is a day left over., the Nameless Day, a time of chaos, a crack between the worlds. The sun was reborn on the solstice as a babe of Cerridwen.
AF

The Wassail

Great honour has been paid to apple trees down the centuries, and in some places still is. In parts of Britain apple trees are wassailed at Yuletide. The trees are visited and cakes or bread soaked in cider are placed in the branches, and cider poured over the roots as a libation. Occasionally roasted apples floating in cider are offered. Sometimes shots are fired to scare away evil spirits from the orchards. The health of the trees is toasted with cider and they are asked to continue to produce abundantly. Trees that are poor bearers of fruit are not honoured. Some suggest that wassailing of the apple at midwinter may be similar to the ancient Druidic custom of cutting the mistletoe, which grows more commonly on apple than oak. The pouring of cider on the roots might replace the more ancient practice of pouring blood on them as a ritual act of fertilisation.

WASSAIL
$2\frac{1}{4}$ pt cider
3 apples, grated
2 oz brown sugar
$\frac{1}{2}$ tsp. ground ginger
Grated nutmeg
Method
Put a $\frac{1}{4}$ pint of cider in a pan and add the grated apples. Cook until the apple is soft and add the brown sugar, ginger and the other 2 pints of cider. Heat through but do not allow to boil. Add some grated nutmeg and pour into a large cup or bowl. This is passed from one person to another with the blessing "Waes haelinch" or 'good health'.
AF

Holly, Ivy, Evergreen
To keep alive the vegetation spirit in the dark days of winter death, houses were decorated with evergreens, holly, ivy and mistletoe. Evergreens had great power as they could withstand the winter death.

The mistletoe was called the druids plant. As it grew not on the ground, but on the branches of a tree it was considered very magical. The berries were regarded as the semen of the host tree, or by some the semen of the Lord of the Trees. The most sacred mistletoe grew on the oak [a rare occurrence].

The oak was the chief tree of the druids and its Celtic name, dur gives both the root of 'druid' and 'door', the oak being both a door to the next season and to the world knowledge. Around the midwinter solstice, preferably on the sixth day of the moon, the druid, would cut the mistletoe from the oak in one stroke with a golden sickle. The mistletoe represented the vitality of the oak and was used to strengthen the sun god in His weakened state.

Amongst the Celts, warfare had to cease at the time of the winter solstice and mistletoe cutting. This is why we see the solstice as a time of peace and goodwill, the Christians adopted this. Formerly Christian cathedrals and churches would lay mistletoe on the alter for the twelve days of Christmas and in some cities, such as York, a general pardon would be proclaimed at the gates.

Trees and evergreens played a large part in the solstice celebrations. In Scandinavian and other northern countries, including some Celtic ones, evergreen trees were decked with lights. The Romans decorated pine trees with images of Bacchus.

The waning half of the year was the season of the Holly King. The custom of holly decoration was carried on into the Christian era although it was not to be brought in until Christmas eve or allowed to remain after twelfth night. The ivy is a symbol of life and rebirth as it remains green throughout the winter and for it's spiral growth.

Though there is little fresh food available at this time, unless it is imported, Yule remains the time of great feasting and merrymaking, when special foods, such as sweets, costly spices, liqueurs and spirits, are brought out to celebrate the rebirth of the sun and impart a little cheer in the depths of winter.

The Druids considered that any elder berries that remained in December were the last gift from the Earth Goddess, and they were ritually gathered and made into potent wine, only to be drunk by initiates to facilitate clairvoyance. The wine was also poured as a libation in sacred places and given to sacrificial victims at the solstices. During the winter the tree represents the Crone and Death aspects of the Goddess. If you can find any berries in December these are a rare and potent gift of the Goddess, and any wine made from them will be a mighty sabbat brew.

MULLED MEAD
1 pt mead
$1/2$ oz bruised ginger
4 cloves
1 cinnamon stick
Method
Heat the mead to no hotter than 60oC with the bruised ginger, cloves cinnamon.

YULE INCENSE
3 parts frankincense
A few drops orange oil
A few drops juniper oil
1 part crushed juniper berries
$1/2$ part mistletoe
Method
Blend together and burn on charcoal.
AF

EVERGREEN
Holly and mistletoe,
Bright amid the green.
Garlanded boughs of fir and pine.
Life within the realm of Nature's Dark Queen.

Reminding us of Summer blooms and the spreading vine.
We drink its promise in the solar glow
Whose dim light is encouraged by the candle flame,
Whose secret strengths we are yet too young to know;
They dwelt in the lost aeons before we mortals came.
PH

Yule Ritual For Two Celebrants

Cast the circle.

Celebrant One: This is the dead time, the end before the beginning. The Lord has entered the Underworld, the Kingdom of Death. This is the time of the Crone.

Celebrant Two: *"Her cloak covers the land."*

Celebrant One: *"In the darkness lie her secrets."*

Celebrant Two: *"In the darkness her secrets are revealed."*

Celebrant One: *"She is the Queen of Mystery"*

Celebrant Two: *"The teacher of secrets."*

The dance and chant takes place:

> *Dance the circle dance of dreaming,*
> *Weaving through the darkling sea,*
> *Spin the web of mist and moonlight,*
> *Come thou, Lady, unto me.*
>
> *Chant the chant of souls entwining,*
> *Round and through the sacred fire,*
> *Drink from wells of mist and moonshine*
> *The cauldron born of true desire.*

Dream the dreams of solemn passion
Through the star encrusted night,
Weave the web of mist and moonfire
Come Lady, come, and share the light.

Hear the tides, the heaving waters,
Sombre on the crystal sand,
Hear the chant of longing, waiting,
Come, fulfil at love's demand.

Seek and know my waiting body,
Mind floating in the deep, dark sea,
Tread the path of mist and moonlight,
Lady, come, beloved, unto me.

Spend time scrying into the crystal or the fire and share the experience. The cakes and wine are shared and the circle is broken.
AF

Yule Pathworking

Relax.

Imagine that you are walking up a hillside just before dawn. It is the night of the winter solstice. Around you the earth and the trees are bare, except for the dark green holly bushes bearing splashes of berries- bright red, vital life in the midst of winter desolation.

As you reach the crown of the hill, you come upon a circle of stones, each bearing quartz crystals. They glint and shine in the pre-dawn light. Inside the ring is a burial mound, its entrance flanked with rocks marked with spirals, the symbol of the passage of the sun around the earth and its daily and yearly death and rebirth.

It is getting light now as you enter the chamber inside the mound. You know it is a burial chamber, but you are not afraid. It seems quite peaceful and a place of promise- more like a womb that a tomb.

Suddenly, a shaft of bright light illuminates the chamber. It is the light of the newly risen sun hitting the tunnel of the mound and shining down onto the inner chamber, filling it with radiance.

You feel the light and warmth on your skin, penetrating the cells of your body, entering the very core of your being. The illumination fills you, revitalising every part of you, making you feel full of life and vitality. You feel the possibilities of life, the newness of everything. With the reborn sun, you are reborn, a child of light and promise. From this point you can make a new beginning and all is possible for you. Take some time to explore this feeling. Bathe in the radiance.

You leave the chamber. Outside morning has begun. A bright, winter light illuminates the landscape. You become aware that the day is fresh and newborn. A new time has begun. Your new energy makes you want to seize the time, to work for what you want in mind, body and spirit. Explore what these are. When you are ready, thank the Gods for your insights and return yourself to waking consciousness.
AF

Solo Yule Ritual

Prepare a sacred place and decorate it with boughs of evergreens - holly, ivy, pine and mistletoe. Hang up symbols of the sun, such as golden discs and globes. On a small table or altar place an unlit candle, some pieces of paper and a pen, a fireproof dish, matches and an incense burner with Yule incense.

Say:

'*This is the time of the winter solstice, when darkness and cold are spread over the land. Yet the time of promise is at hand, when the sun shall be reborn, and the days will grow longer and brighter from this point. The Child of Light shall come.*'

Meditate for a while on the season. Consider what is happening to you at this time, how the season affects you, what you hope for in the future. What stops you achieving your spiritual and personal goals? What fears? What inhibitions? What bad habits?

Take the pen and paper and write down those parts of yourself you wish to be rid of, each on a separate piece of paper.

Take the matches and light the candle, saying:

'*Let this flame symbolise the light of the waxing sun and the promise of the New Year. Let it be the light of love and joy within me.*'

Take each piece of paper and burn it in the flame, visualising each thing burning away in the fire, leaving you free. Say:

"*As this candle burns, let all goodness enter herein, and let all negativity be burned away. With this New Year I am reborn, a child of light and promise.*"

Close the right and let the candle burn down.
AF

Yuletide in a Modern World

In these modern times the commercial signs of Christmas appear in early November: we are exhorted to spend out money. As the days grow shorter, so does our patience with all the fuss. Many people now do not dwell on the Christian significance of the occasion, nor does it necessarily become the season of goodwill. Rather it is about having to find the cash for what is expected. But that is a cynical view; naturally, we like to give to those we love, and to our friends of any kind. We are increasing our companionship in the shorter, darker days, building the closeness of human affection in the gathering cold and the weakening of the life-giving sun. Perhaps, without knowing, people seek the comfort of the Mother's embrace. The Earth Mother holds her children now as in the beginning of all life on earth; as the Cosmic Mother's spiral arms encompass and cherish the Universe.

Her time is not just the present, but the Eternal Moment; which we all know, but which in everyday consciousness is expressed in time's constantly moving images. Her awareness is not only of Earth's differing religions, but the One expression of everlasting Love. The stars glow in the darkness of Mystery, from which their light is born, from which our Sun is born.

In sorrow it is so easy to forget that the concept of the Cosmic Being is not of separation, that all journeys in time simply expand the consciousness of the beginning, that the place of pilgrimage is the focus of the journey's start, not just another place. At Yule, and in other particular points of the wheel of the year, people often care to focus on holy places, their emotions lean towards Home. The original home of all of us is the universe's beginning, but it will still be there at the cosmic end. Our life's journey is an outward travelling of the spirit, the consciousness, the emotions, the mind, even if we never leave the land, town or village of our birth.

In both Pagan and Christian thought, the Lord of Light is born at Yule. Whether we dwell on the Dark Mother of Mystery, who is also mistress of death and rebirth, or perceive the humanity/divinity of the mother of the Christ child, we see light from darkness [or lesser awareness], life from death, spring from winter.

We are material creatures and it never stops being a material universe. We feel the touch of the distant sun, although it hides at night, but then we are in the embrace of Arianrhod, Goddess of the Moon, whose power draws together the waters of the seas.
PH

Group Rite For Yule

The circle is decorated with holly, ivy, mistletoe and evergreens. All the lights are extinguished. The oak fire is lit from the remains of last year's Yule Log. The circle is cast.

High Priestess : "*In this the season of the Dark Time, shrouded in the cloak of the Crone, we celebrate the festival of Yule, the rebirth of the sun, and the life of the coming year. Queen of the midnight skies, Mistress of Death, Keeper of the Spiral Castle of Rebirth, we call upon you this night. Mother of the Light, descend I beseech thee.*"

Each person takes a token, usually the remains of last year's mistletoe, and invokes into it all that they wish to pass away with the year, such as negative feelings, pain, bad habits, old ties and so on. This is then burned in the fire. Each person is purified with juniper smoke :

High Priestess : "*May we be purified, ready to greet the Lord as He is reborn, ready to greet the waxing year.*"

Drumming and chanting begins to work up energy. Fire jumping purifies. When ready the North Tree is decorated by each person with solar symbols to encourage the sun. Each person in turn lights a candle from the North beacon to symbolise their hopes for the coming year. Candles for friends and families may also be lit. Mistletoe is bound in red thread to symbolise the fertility of the Lord of the Forest, which will be used to strengthen the new born Sun. A piece is given to each group member to hang over their doors all year round as a sign of hospitality, and which will be burned the next Yule.

High Priest :
> *"Queen of heaven, moon and night,*
> *Water, air and fire and earth,*
> *Widowed Queen, return the One*
> *Bring the light unto its birth.*
> *Queen of sadness, grieving woe*
> *Queen of future, Queen of bane,*
> *Queen that guards the new and past,*
> *Grant that light return again.*
> *Rise O child and new beginning*
> *Show thy light to all the world*
> *Light above the land and ocean*
> *Be the veil of darkness furled*
> *Blessed is the Triple Mother*
> *Queen of Dark and Queen of Day*
> *Hers the dance and Hers rejoicing,*
> *AP-AP-AN-O-IR-UT-AY."*

The man chosen to represent the Sun King is reborn from beneath the cloak of the Mother, the High Priestess.

High Priestess: [Giving him the sword] "*Be thou armed to conquer the dark*" [Crowning him with mistletoe] "*May you grow in strength.*" [Draping Him with a red sash] "*May the year grow with you.*" [Giving him the lit beacon] "*The light is reborn!*"

The Sun King passes round the circle from North to West to North again, saluting each quarter of the circle in turn. He plants the beacon in the North of the circle.

High Priest : "*The Dark God has passed through the underworld and has been reborn as the Sun Child from the womb of the Mother. With Him we are each reborn. Blessed Be!*"

All : "*BLESSED BE.*"

The cakes and wine are blessed and shared. The circle is broken which is a signal for the joyful feasting to begin.
AF

FREE DETAILED CATALOGUE

Capall Bann is owned and run by people actively involved in many of the areas in which we publish. A detailed illustrated catalogue is available on request, SAE or International Postal Coupon appreciated. **Titles can be ordered direct from Capall Bann, post free in the UK** (cheque or PO with order) or from good bookshops and specialist outlets.

Do contact us for details on the latest releases at: **Capall Bann Publishing, Freshfields, Chieveley, Berks, RG20 8TF.** Titles include:

Arthur - The Legend Unveiled, C Johnson & E Lung
Asyniur - Womens Mysteries in the Northern Tradition, S McGrath
Begonnings - Geomancy, Builder's Rites & Electional Astrology in the European Tradition, Nigel Pennick
Between Earth and Sky, Julia Day
Call of the Horned Piper, Nigel Jackson
Celtic Faery Shamanism, Catrin James
Celtic Faery Shamanism - The Wisdom of the Otherworld, Catrin James
Celtic Lore & Druidic Ritual, Rhiannon Ryall
Celtic Sacifice - Pre Christian Ritual & Religion, Marion Pearce
Celtic Saints and the Glastonbury Zodiac, Mary Caine
Circle and the Square, Jack Gale
Compleat Vampyre - The Vampyre Shaman, Nigel Jackson
Creating Form From the Mist - The Wisdom of Women in Celtic Myth and Culture, Lynne Sinclair-Wood
Crystal Clear - A Guide to Quartz Crystal, Jennifer Dent
Crystal Doorways, Simon & Sue Lilly
Dragons of the West, Nigel Pennick
Earth Dance - A Year of Pagan Rituals, Jan Brodie
Earth Harmony - Places of Power, Holiness & Healing, Nigel Pennick
Earth Magic, Margaret McArthur
Enchanted Forest - The Magical Lore of Trees, Yvonne Aburrow
Eternal Priestess, Sage Weston
Eternally Yours Faithfully, Roy Radford & Evelyn Gregory
Everything You Always Wanted To Know About Your Body, But So Far Nobody's Been Able To Tell You, Chris Thomas & D Baker
Face of the Deep - Healing Body & Soul, Penny Allen
Fairies in the Irish Tradition, Molly Gowen
Familiars - Animal Powers of Britain, Anna Franklin
Forest Paths - Tree Divination, Brian Harrison, Ill. S. Rouse
God Year, The, Nigel Pennick & Helen Field

Goddess on the Cross, Dr George Young
Goddess Year, The, Nigel Pennick & Helen Field
Handbook For Pagan Healers, Liz Joan
Handbook of Fairies, Ronan Coghlan
Healing Book, The, Chris Thomas and Diane Baker
Healing Homes, Jennifer Dent
Healing Journeys, Paul Williamson
Healing Stones, Sue Philips
Herb Craft - Shamanic & Ritual Use of Herbs, Lavender & Franklin
In Search of Herne the Hunter, Eric Fitch
Inner Celtia, Alan Richardson & David Annwn
Legend of Robin Hood, The, Richard Rutherford-Moore
Lid Off the Cauldron, Patricia Crowther
Light From the Shadows - Modern Traditional Witchcraft, Gwyn
Living Tarot, Ann Walker
Lore of the Sacred Horse, Marion Davies
Lost Lands & Sunken Cities (2nd ed.), Nigel Pennick
Magic of Herbs - A Complete Home Herbal, Rhiannon Ryall
Magical Guardians - Exploring the Spirit and Nature of Trees, Philip Heselton
Magical History of the Horse, Janet Farrar & Virginia Russell
Magical Lore of Animals, Yvonne Aburrow
Magical Lore of Cats, Marion Davies
Magical Lore of Herbs, Marion Davies
Magick Without Peers, Ariadne Rainbird & David Rankine
Masks of Misrule - Horned God & His Cult in Europe, Nigel Jackson
Medicine For The Coming Age, Lisa Sand MD
Menopausal Woman on the Run, Jaki da Costa
Menopause and the Emotions, Kathleen I Macpherson
Mind Massage - 60 Creative Visualisations, Marlene Maundrill
Mirrors of Magic - Evoking the Spirit of the Dewponds, P Heselton
Moon Mysteries, Jan Brodie
Mysteries of the Runes, Michael Howard
New Celtic Oracle The, Nigel Pennick & Nigel Jackson
Pagan Feasts - Seasonal Food for the 8 Festivals, Franklin & Phillips
Patchwork of Magic - Living in a Pagan World, Julia Day
Pathworking - A Practical Book of Guided Meditations, Pete Jennings
Personal Power, Anna Franklin
Pickingill Papers - The Origins of Gardnerian Wicca, Bill Liddell
Practical Divining, Richard Foord
Practical Meditation, Steve Hounsome
Practical Spirituality, Steve Hounsome
Psychic Self Defence - Real Solutions, Jan Brodie
Real Fairies, David Tame
Reality - How It Works & Why It Mostly Doesn't, Rik Dent
Romany Tapestry, Michael Houghton
Runic Astrology, Nigel Pennick

Sacred Animals, Gordon MacLellan
Sacred Celtic Animals, Marion Davies, Ill. Simon Rouse
Sacred Dorset - On the Path of the Dragon, Peter Knight
Sacred Grove - The Mysteries of the Forest, Yvonne Aburrow
Sacred Geometry, Nigel Pennick
Sacred Ring - Pagan Origins of British Folk Festivals, M. Howard
Season of Sorcery - On Becoming a Wisewoman, Poppy Palin
Seasonal Magic - Diary of a Village Witch, Paddy Slade
Secret Places of the Goddess, Philip Heselton
Secret Signs & Sigils, Nigel Pennick
Spirits of the Air, Jaq D Hawkins
Spirits of the Earth, Jaq D Hawkins
Spirits of the Earth, Jaq D Hawkins
Stony Gaze, Investigating Celtic Heads John Billingsley
Stumbling Through the Undergrowth , Mark Kirwan-Heyhoe
Symbols of Ancient Gods, Rhiannon Ryall
Talking to the Earth, Gordon MacLellan
Taming the Wolf - Full Moon Meditations, Steve Hounsome
Teachings of the Wisewomen, Rhiannon Ryall
The Other Kingdoms Speak, Helena Hawley
Tree: Essence of Healing, Simon & Sue Lilly
Tree: Essence, Spirit & Teacher, Simon & Sue Lilly
Through the Veil, Peter Paddon
Torch and the Spear, Patrick Regan
Understanding Chaos Magic, Jaq D Hawkins
Vortex - The End of History, Mary Russell
Warriors at the Edge of Time, Jan Fry
Water Witches, Tony Steele
Way of the Magus, Michael Howard
Weaving a Web of Magic, Rhiannon Ryall
West Country Wicca, Rhiannon Ryall
Wildwitch - The Craft of the Natural Psychic, Poppy Palin
Wildwood King , Philip Kane
Witches of Oz, Matthew & Julia Philips
Wondrous Land - The Faery Faith of Ireland by Dr Kay Mullin
Working With the Merlin, Geoff Hughes

FREE detailed catalogue and FREE 'Inspiration' magazine
Contact: Capall Bann Publishing, Freshfields, Chieveley, Berks, RG20 8TF